The Entertainment of His Most Excellent Majestie Charles II, in His Passage Through the City of London to His Coronation

HONI SOIT QVI MAL I PENSE

DIEV ET MON DROIT.

THE
ENTERTAINMENT
OF
His Moſt Excellent MAJESTIE

CHARLES II,
IN
His PASSAGE through the CITY of

LONDON
TO HIS
CORONATION:

Containing an exaět Accompt of the whole *Solemnity*; the Triumphal
Arches, and *Cavalcade*, delineated in *Sculpture*; the *Speeches* and
Impreſſes illuſtrated from *Antiquity*.

TO THESE IS ADDED,
A Brief Narrative of His MAJESTIE'S Solemn CORONATION:
WITH
His Magnificent PROCEEDING, and ROYAL FEAST
IN
VVESTMINSTER-HALL.

By *JOHN OGILBY.*

LONDON,
Printed by THO: ROYCROFT, and are to be had at the Authors Houſe
in *Kings-Head* Court within Shoe-Lane, MDCLXII.

I Have perused a brief Narrative of His MAJESTIES Solemn CO-RONATION, printed by Mr OGILBY, together with his Description of His MAJESTIES Entertainment passing through the City of LONDON to His Coronation, &c. and, in pursuance of His MAJESTIES Order unto me directed, have examined, and do approve thereof, so as the said Mr OGILBY may freely publish the same.

From the HERALDS-COLLEDG this thirteenth of June 1662.

EDVVARD WALKER,
Garter Principal King
of Arms.

TO THE

SACRED MAJESTY

OF

CHARLES II,

King of *ENGLAND, SCOTLAND, FRANCE,*
and *IRELAND,* &c.

This DESCRIPTION of the SOLEMNITY of His
Bleſſed INAUGURATION

Is humbly Dedicated

By

His moſt Obedient, Dutiful, and

Loyal Servant,

J. OGILBY.

Wenceslaus Hollar Bohemus delineavit, et aqua forti æri insculpsit. 1661.

2 Munday the 22 of April. A° M.DC.LXI.
foure such Squadrons,   & each Squadron containing fiftie men

3   Squires to the Knights of the Bath,

4   Knights Harbingers   Sewers of the Chamber &   Gentlemen Vshers. Quarter Waiters
        Serjeant Porter

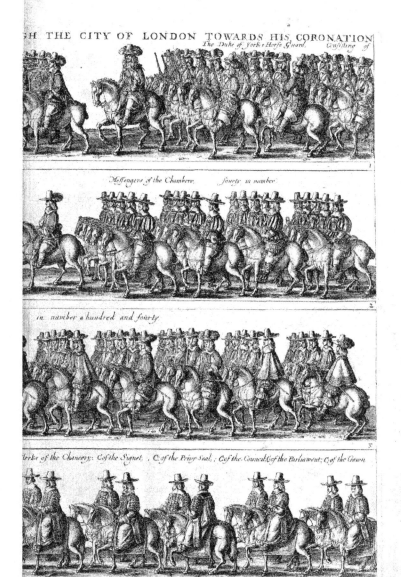

GH THE CITY OF LONDON TOWARDS HIS CORONATION

The Duke of Yorks Horse Guard.   Consisting of

Messengers of the Chambere.   fourty in number.

in number a hundred and fourty.

Clerke of the Chancery: C. of the Signet.   C. of the Privy Seal. : C. of the Councel. C. of the Parliament: C. of the Crown.

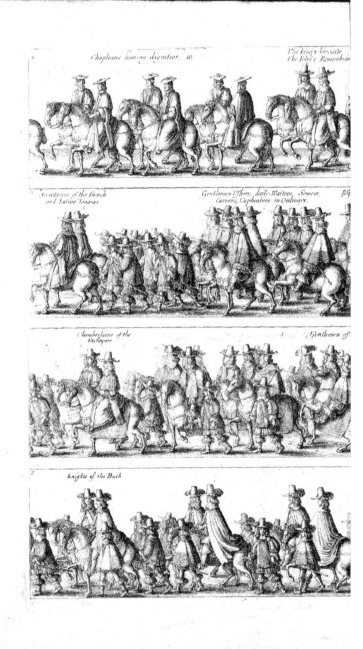

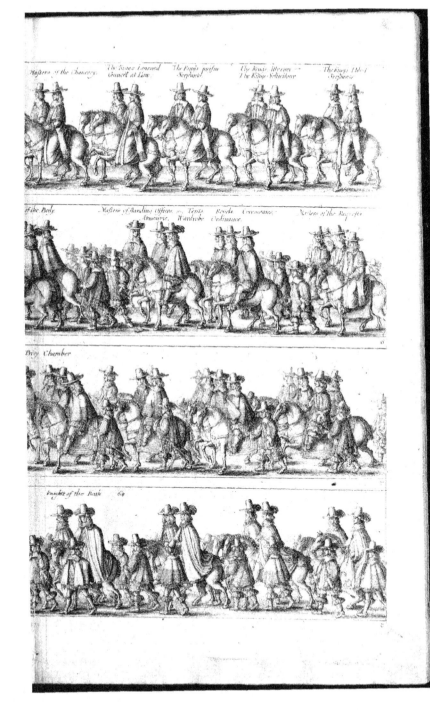

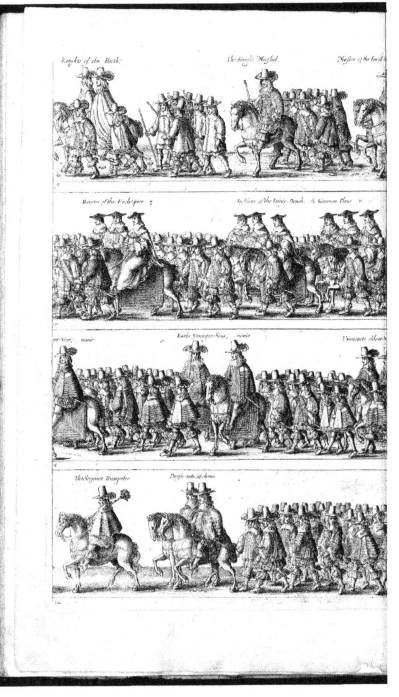

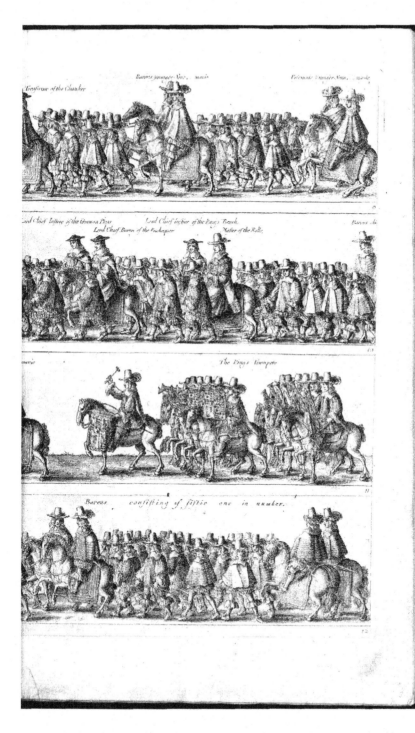

Treasurer of the Chamber   Barons younger Sons.   servis   Viscounts younger Sons.   servis

Lord Chief Justice of the Common Pleas   Lord Chief Justice of the Kings Bench.   Barons &c.
     Lord Chief Baron of the Exchequer   Master of the Rolls.

    servis   The Kings Trumpets

       Barons   consisting of fiftie one in number.

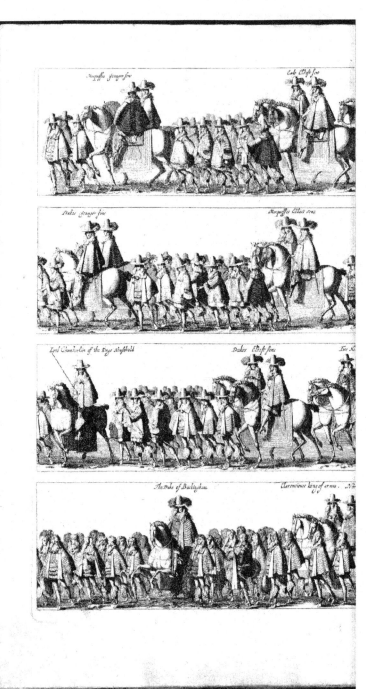

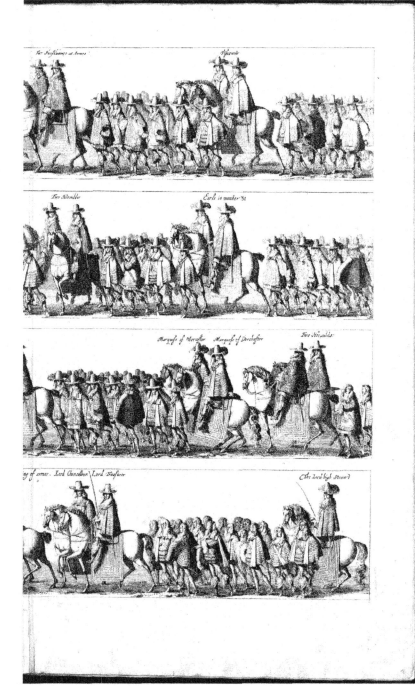

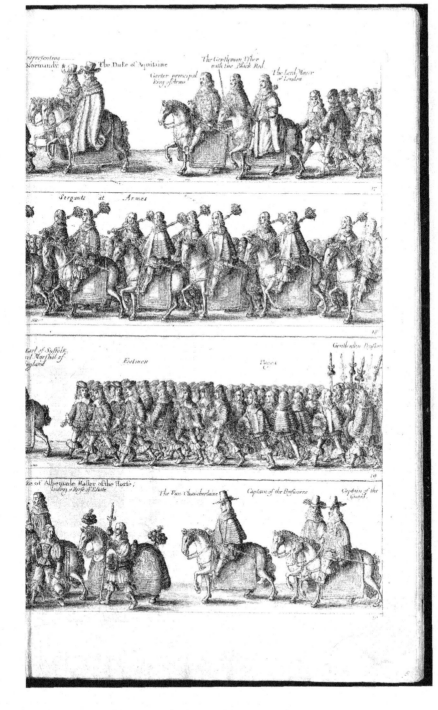

His Majesties
ENTERTAINMENTS
Passing through the City of

LONDON
TO HIS
CORONATION;
WITH
A Description of the Triumphal Arches,
and Solemnity.

THE City of *LONDON*, participating the
greatest share of that inexpressible Happiness,
which these Kingdoms have received by the
glorious Restauration of our Sovereign to His
Throne, and of us His Subjects to our Laws,
Liberties, and Religion, after a dismal Night of
Usurpation, and Oppression, and proportiona-
bly exceeding in their Loyalty, took the occasi-
on of His *MAJESTIES* Coronation, to express their Joy with
the greatest Magnificence imaginable: imitating therein the antient
Romanes, who, at the return of their Emperours, erected *Arches* of
Marble, which though we, by reason of the shortness of Time, could not

B   equal

equal in Materials, yet do ours far exceed theirs in Number, and stupendious Proportions.

THE Custom of erecting *Triumphal Arches* among the *Romans* (a thing altogether unknown to the *Gracians*, till their acquaintance with them) most certainly was not coæval with their *Triumphs*, which were within four years as long-liv'd as *Rome* it self. For among the *Greek*, and *Latin* Authours of the *Roman* History, who have been so accurate in enumerating all their *Solemnities*, especially which concerned their Splendour, and Magnificence, we find not any mention of them till the time of the *Roman* Emperours. Indeed of *Triumphs*, as of all other things, the Beginnings seem to have been but rude. At first nothing more then the Spoils hung up at the house of the Conquerour.

Æneid. VII.   *Virgil*, speaking of the Palace of King *Picus*,

> *Multáque prætereà sacris in postibus arma,*
> *Captivi pendent currus, curvæque secures,*
> *Et Cristæ capitum, & portarum ingentia claustra,*
> *Spiculáque, clypeíque, ereptáque rostra carinis.*

> " Besides, on sacred Pillars all along,
> " A World of Arms, Axes, and Chariots hung,
> " Crests, and huge Bars of Gates the Ports adorn,
> " And Spears, and Shields, and Prows from Gallies torn.

This rudeness of the first *Triumphs*, even among the *Romans*, will sufficiently appear, if we compare the *Triumph* of *Romulus*, mention'd by *Livy, Dionysius Halicarnassensis*, and *Plutarch*, with the excessive Pomp, and Magnificence of the latter, of which we shall give an instance in this Discourse. The greatest Monument of which Magnificence, the *Triumphal Arches*, as we have said, was not heard of before *Julius Cæsar*. 'Tis true, there is still retain'd at *Rome* the memory of *Arcus Romuli*, and *Camilli*. But 'tis certain, it appears not whether they were *Triumphal Arches*, or no; and it is very questionable, whether they bear their true Titles. For *Pliny*, who flourish'd in the time of *Vespasian* the Emperour, calls them *novitium inventum, a new invention*: whose Authority much out-weighs those empty Titles of *Arcus Romuli*, and

Lib. I.
Lib. I I.
in Romulo.

Nat: Hist:
Lib. xxxviii.
cap. vi.

and *Camilli*, of which there is no ancient Record. Yet, that they were in uſe before *Julius Cæſar* almoſt one Century of years, ha's been conjectured out of theſe words of *Aſconius Pedianus* , an *Authour*, againſt whom there is no exception , and who liv'd ſome years before *Pliny*; *Fornix Fabianus, arcus eſt juxta Regiam in Sacra via, à Fabio Cenſore conſtructus, qui, à devictis Allobrogibus,* Allobrox *cognominatus eſt, ibique ſtatua ejus poſita propterea eſt; The Fabian Arch is nigh the* Palace *of Romulus in the Sacred way, built by Fabius the Cenſor, who, from his Victory over the Allobroges, had the ſirname of* Allobrox ; *for which his Statue was placed there.* That he triumph'd upon this Victory, we have ample teſtimony from the Marbles not long ſince digg'd up at *Rome,* formerly preſerved in the *Capitol.* Nevertheleſs, thoſe words of *Aſconius* do evidently conclude the contrary : for he ſays expreſly *built by Fabius Cenſour.* His Cenſourſhip is referred by *Sigonius* and *Pighius* to the Year U.C. DCXLV. his Triumph happened *anno* DCXXXIII. as appears from the Marbles now mention'd,

Q. FABIUS Q. ÆMILIANI F. Q. N. AN. DCXXXIII.

MAXIMUS. PROCOS. DE. ALLOBROgibus

ET. REGE. ARVERNORUM. BETULTO. X. K·

Whence it is clear the Arch was built long after his Triumph. And I conceive his Statue was plac'd there rather in regard of his expences, then of his Victory ſo long before obtain'd. Neither is it ſtrange after the ſpace of above ſeven hundred years , to find this alteration. We may obſerve many other , but ſhall onely take notice of two. Firſt, The ancient *Romans* granted not the honour of Triumph to any, who had not ſlain in one pitch'd Field five thouſand of their Enemies. *Jus triumphi datur ei, qui quinque millia hoſtium unà acie ceciderit.* Secondly, They allowed not Triumph for a Victory over their Fellow-Citizens; as *Q. Catulus* triumph'd not over *M. Lepidus,* or *L. Antony* over *Catilin,* or *Sylla* over *Marius,* or *Cinna* over *Carbo,* or *Cæſar* over *Pompey.*

Valer Maximus. Lib II. cap viii.

Claudian,

—— *cùm Gallica vulgò*
Prælia jactaret, tacuit Pharſalica Cæſar,
Namq; inter ſocias acies, cognataq́ ſigna,
Ut vinci miſerum, nunquam viciſſe decorum.

De vi. Conſulatu Honorii.

Of

—— Of *Gallick* Fights oft at his Board
Boasts *Cæsar*, of *Pharsalia* not a word.
Though sad the case to fall in Civil War,
Yet 'tis no honour to the Conquerour.

which he means too in these Verses,

De Bello
Gilico

Semperab his famæ petiere insignia bellis,
Quæ diversa, procul tuto, trans æquora virtus
Exercere dabat : currus, Regiónque catenæ
Inter abundantis fati ludibria ductæ.

They by such Wars sought Fame in Fields remote,
Beyond Seas Victory by their Valour got :
Hence Kings in Chains and Chariots march in state,
'Mongst various Sports of their abundant Fate.

Ibid.

Liv. Lib. xl.

De civibus triumphare nefas, saith the same *Valerius Maximus*. In both
which particulars the *Roman* History affords exceptions. In the first,
in the *Triumph without a War*, anno *Urbis Cond.* D L X X I I I.   In the
second, in the Triumphal Arch, yet almost entirely standing, of *Constan-*
tine the Great, which the Senate, and People of *Rome* dedicated to him
upon his Victory over *Maxentius*, a General of part of the Imperial
Forces. The Inscription this,

IMP. CÆS. FL. CONSTANTINO. MAXIMO
P. F. AUGUSTO S. P. Q. R.
QUOD. INSTINCTU. DIVINITATIS. MENTIS
MAGNITUDINE. CUM. EXERCITU. SUO.
TAM. DE. TYRANNO. QUAM DE OMNI EJUS
TACTIONE. UNO. TEMPORE. JUSTIS
REMPUBLICAM. ULTUS. EST. ARMIS
ARCUM. TRIUMPHIS· INSIGNEM. DICAVIT

Three

Three *Triumphs*, of the same nature, in one Century of years, are *De vi. Con-*
reckoned by *Claudian*, who makes *Rome* to speak thus, *sulatu Hono-*
rii.

> *His annis, qui lustra mihi bis dena recensent,*
> *Nostra ter Augustos intra pomæria vidi,*
> *Temporibus variis: eadem sed causa Tropæis,*
> *Civilis dissensus erat ———*

> Lustres twice ten, with annual Springs, and Falls,
> Pass'd, since I saw three Emp'rours in our Walls,
> At sev'ral times : each, on sad Scores, did boast
> Triumphs for Civil Broils ———

Both which particulars comprehend this *Triumph* of His most *Sacred*
Majesty, which was upon a Victory over the Enemies of His Countrey without a Battle.

These *Arches* generally bore the name of him, that rid in Triumph,
and had a Title insculp'd, to testifie for what Victory they were erected :
both which appear from this Speech of the City of *Rome* to *Honorius*
the Emperour,

> *Ast ego frænabam geminos, quibus altior ires,* *Claudian ib.*
> *Electi candoris equos, & nominis Arcum*
> *Jam molita tui, per quem radiante decorus*
> *Ingrederere togâ, pugnæ monumenta dicabam*
> *Defensam titulo Libyam testata perenni.*

> But I put in your Steeds more white then Snow,
> And of your Name design'd a stately Arch,
> Through which you might in Regal Purple march.
> The Battle too, and lasting claim engrav'd
> Attesting Monuments that you *Libya* sav'd.

They were always adorn'd with some Spoils of the Conquered Enemy. *Claudian*,

> ——— *Spoliisque micantes*   *Pan g iv.*
> *Innumeros arcus* ———

                    C   Innum'rous

Innum'rous Arches rich with glitt'ring Spoils.

Prudentius,

> *Frustrà igitur currus summo miramur in Arcu*
> *Quadrijugos, stantésque Duces in curribus altis,*
> *Sub pedibusque Ducum captivos poplite flexo*
> *Ad juga depressos, manibusque in terga retortis,*
> *Et suspensa gravi telorum fragmina trunco.*

We Chariots on the Arch admire in vain,
In them their haughty Leaders standing see,
And Captives stooping with low-bended knee,
Their hands behind them ti'd; of pond'rous Oke
Huge Truncheons hanging of strong Jav'lins broke.

Sometimes they bore insculp'd the Battle, in which the Conquerour had merited his *Triumph*, as those of *Septimius Severus*, and *Constantine*. In others, the whole pomp of the *Triumph* was represented; as in that of *Vespasian* and *Titus*, where are still to be seen led in *Triumph* the Spoils of the Temple of *Jerusalem*, the Ark of the Covenant, the Candlestick with seven Branches, the Table of the Shew-Bread, the Tables of the Decalogue, with the Vessels of pure Gold for the use of the Temple, the Captives chain'd, the Emperour riding in his *Triumphal* Chariot, &c. The order, and method of a *Triumph*, among the *Romans*, we will here briefly, but distinctly deliver, chiefly out of *Plutarch*, in the Life of *P. Æmilius.*

In Romulo. The captivated Statues, Pictures, and Colossusses, lead the Van. *Plutarch*, of the Triumph of *P. Æmilius*, *The first day* (for this Triumph lasted three) *scarce sufficed for the passing of the Statues, Pictures, and Colosses, lead in two hundred and fifty Carriages.* *Appian* says, that *Pompey* carried the Statues of the Forreign Gods in Triumph.

The next followed the choicest Arms and Spoils of the Enemy. Plutarch, *The next day were carried the fairest and richest of the* Macedonian *Weapons upon several Carriages, glistering with the Brass and Iron new scowr'd: artificially plac'd, (yet that they seem'd to have been thrown together promiscuously without any order) the Head-pieces upon the Shields, the Corslets upon the Buskins,* &c. *which striking constantly against each other, made so terrible a noise, that the sight of them, though now overcome, was a terrour to the Spectatours.* Statius,

                                                          Ante

Ante Ducem spolia, & duri Mavortis imago,   Lib. xii.
Virginei currus, cumulatáque fercula cristis,
Et tristes ducuntur equi. ———

The Gen'ral, Spoils, and *Mars* dire Shape precedes
Chariots and Chargers heap'd with Crests, and Steeds
Mourning are led
Ovid,

Scuta sed & galeæ gemmis radientur & auro,   De Ponto, Lib. iii. Eleg. iv.
Sténtque super victos trunca tropæa viros.

But Gems, and Gold their Shields, and Helms adorn,
The Trophies on the vanquish'd Shoulders born.

Next, the Images of the Cities, Towns, Castles, Mountains, and
Rivers, taken. *Ovid,*   De Tristib. Lib. iv. Eleg. ii.

Cumque Ducum titulis oppida capta leget :
Hic lacus, hi montes, hæc tot castella, tot urbes,
Plena feræ cædis, plena cruoris erant.

There taken Towns, and Princes Titles read :
There Lakes, there Mountains, Forts, and Cities stood;
Full with dire Slaughter, full of Purple Blood.

Protinùs, argento veros imitantia muros,
Barbara cum victis oppida lata viris :

Flumináque in montes, & in altas proflua sylvas,
Armaque cum telis in strue juncta suis.

Next, Barb'rous Cities with the Captives past
True Walls resembling in pure Silver cast :
And Rivers that 'mongst Woods and Mountains glide,
And Arms, and Weapons, rais'd like Trophies, ride.

Livy * says, that *Scipio Asiaticus* carried in Triumph the Images of an   * Lib. xxxviii. † Nat. Hist. Lib. v. Cap. v.
hundred and thirty four Towns. *Pliny* † reckons up twenty seven Ci-
ties,

ties, Towns, Nations, Mountains, &c. led before *Cornelius Balbus.* *Silius Italicus,* of the Triumph of *Scipio Africanus* over *Carthage.*

Mox victas tendens Carthago *ad sidera palmas*
Ibat, & effigies oræ jam lenis Iberæ,
Terrarum finis Gades, *ac laudibus olim*
Terminus Herculeis Calpe, *Bætisque lavare*
Solis equos dulci consuetus fluminis undâ,
Frondosumque apicem subigens ad sidera mater
Bellorum fera Pyrene, *nec mitis* Iberus,
Cùm simul illidit Ponto *quos attulit amnes.*

———— Next, lifting to
The Stars her Conquer'd hands, did *Carthage* go,
Then the Effigies of th' *Iberian* Land,
Now Peaceable; with *Gades,* that doth stand
The Period of the Earth; and *Calpe,*that,
Of old, *Alcides* praise did terminate :
With *Bætis,* which the Horses of the Sun
Is wont to bathe in Streams that gently run :
And high *Pyrene,* which gives Birth to Wars,
And lifts her heavy Head unto the Stars:
With rude *Iberus,* that with Fury flings
Against the Sea the Rivers, that he brings.

Mr. ROSS.

Then followed the Moneys of Silver, Vessels, Garments, &c. Plutarch, *After which, three thousand men carrying the Moneys of Silver in seven hundred and fifty Silver Vessels; each of them weighing three Talents, four men to a Vessel.*

Next the Trumpeters. Plutarch, *The next day betimes in the Morning went the Trumpeters founding a Charge.* After whom were led the Oxen ordain'd for Sacrifice. Livy, *The Victimes, which go before, are not the least part of the Triumph.* These were white, taken out of the Medows of the River *Clitumnus.* Virgil,

Hinc

Hinc albi, Clitumne, greges, & maxima taurus   Geerg. l.
Victima, sæpe tuo perfusi flumine sacro,
Romanos ad Templa Deûm duxère Triumphos.

This snowy Flocks, and Bulls prime Off'rings yields,
Which bath'd, *Clitumnus*, in thy Sacred Floods,
Rome's Triumphs draw to Temples of the Gods.

Upon which place *Servius*, Clitumnus *is a River in* Menavia, *which is a part of* Umbria, *as* Umbria *is of* Tuscia, *whence whatsoever Beasts drink, they bring forth their young ones white.*   Claudian,

    Quin & Clitumni sacras victoribus undas,   Panegyr. iv.
    Candida quæ Latiis præbent armenta Triumphis.

    Clitumnus sacred Streams, whose Snow-white Breed
    The conqu'ring *Romans* in their Triumphs need.
Ovid,

    Candidáque adductâ collum percussa securi   De Tristi-
bus, lib. iv.
Eleg. ii.
    Victima purpureo sanguine tingit humum.

    Struck with an Axe the pure white Sacrifice
    Earth with a purple River dies.

Next the Gold, and Golden Vessels, taken from the Enemy.   Plutarch, *After the Sacrifices went those that carried the Gold, divided, as the Silver was, into Vessels, weighing each three Talents, the number of the Vessels, seventy seven: with those that carried the Sacred Cup, which* Æmilius *had caus'd to be made of ten Talents of Gold, adorn'd with several pretious Stones,* &c.
Then followed the Arms of the Conquered Prince. *After which he sent the Chariot of* Perseus, *and his Arms, and his Crown plac'd upon his Arms.*
Next the Captives, richly clad, but laden with Chains; the Captive Prince with Chains of Gold, the rest according to their quality. Silius Italicus,

    Ante Siphax feretro residens captiva premebat   Lib. xvii.
    Lumina, & auratæ servabant colla catenæ.
    Hic Hanno, clarique genus Phænissa juventa,
    Ei Macedum primi, atque incocti corpora Mauri,
                      D   *Tunc*

Tum Nomades, notúsque sacro, cùm lustrat arenas,
Hammoni Garamas : &c.
Sed non ulla magis mentésque oculósque tenebat,
Quàm visa Hannibalis campis fugientis imago.

——Before him *Siphax,* Captivate,
Upon a Beere, his Eyes dejected, sate,
His Neck in Golden Chains preserv'd.   And here
Hanno, and young *Phœnician* Nobles were ;
Then *Macedonian* Princes ; next to these
The *Moors* with parched Skins ; then *Nomades*
And *Garamantians* known to Horned *Jove ,*
Where they the Sands survey, *&c.*
Yet nothing more delights their Mind, and Eyes,
Then *Hannibal,* as in the Field he flies,

                                        Mr. ROSS.

Propertius,

Lib. vj.
El. jc.

     Aut Regum auratis circumdata colla catenis,
       Actiáque in Sacra currere rostra via.

Or else their Kings in Golden Fetters bound ;
The Sacred way with *Actian* Wheels resound.

Ovid,

De arte Am.

     Ibant antè duces onerati colla catenis.

Before, the Princes went in Golden Chains.

Trebellius, speaking of Queen *Zenobia, Jam primùm ornata gemmis ingentibus, itá ut ornamentorum onere laboraret : vincti erant pedes auro, manus etiam catenis aureis, nec collo aureum vinculum deerat.* She was now so deck'd with great Gems, that she was oppress'd with the weight of her Ornaments: her Feet, Hands, and Neck were bound with Chains.   But this was not constant : for in a Triumph of *Pompey's Appian* mentions a great number of Captives, οὐδὲν δεδεμένος, but *none bound.*

Next followed the Crowns, which the Cities, Friends of the *Romans,* had presented to the General. *Virgil,*

                                        Ipse

Ipse sedens niveo candentis limine Phœbi
Dona recognoscit sociorum, aptátque superbis
Postibus.———

He in bright Porches of great *Phœbus* sits,
And gifts of Nations to proud Pillars fits.

Plutarch, *After which were carried* 400. *Golden Crown's, which the Cities had sent to* Paulus Æmilius *by their Ambassadours, as a reward of his Victory.*

Next, he that rid in Triumph, in his Triumphal habit, elegantly described by *Juvenal.*   *Sat.* 8.

Quid si vidisset Prætorem in curribus altis
Exstantem, & medio sublimem in pulvere Circi
In tunica Jovis, *& pictæ Sarrana ferentem*
Ex humeris aulæa togæ, magnæque Coronæ
Tantum orbem quanto cervix non sufficit ulla?
Quippe tenet sudans hanc publicus, & sibi Consul
Nè placeat, curru servus portatur eodem.
Da nunc & volucrem sceptro quæ surgit eburno,
Illinc Cornicines, hinc præcedentia longi
Agminis officia, & niveos ad fræna Quirites,
Defossa in loculis quos sportula fecit amicos.

Had he the *Prætor* in his Chariot spi'd
Amidst the dusty *Cirque* in Triumph ride,
In *Joves* bright Vest, in an imbroider'd Gown
Of *Tyrian* Purple, and a mighty Crown,
For any Head too weighty, and too large,
That is forsooth a sweating Servants charge:
Least that the *Consul* in such pomp should pride,
The Slave and he both in one Chariot ride.
On th' Ivory Scepter th' Eagle seen displai'd,
Here Cornets, there his friendly Cavalcade;
Romans in white march neer the Horses Reins,
Friends by the Basket and their Belly-gains.

The Army followed the Chariot of their General. Plutarch, *The whole Army was crown'd with Lawrel, following the Chariot of their General in their ranks, and orders.* Who usually sang Io TRIUMPHE. *Ovid,* speaking of the Triumph of *Drusus Germanicus*;

> *Tempora Phœbeâ lauro cingentur,* Ioque
> Miles, Io *magnâ voce* TRIUMPHE, *canet.*

Io the Army with fresh Lawrel Crown'd
Io TRIUMPHE as they march resound.

De Imâ Sti-licons. Claudian,

> *Ipse albis veheretur equis, currumque secutus,*
> *Laurigerum festo fremuisset carmine miles.*

Drawn with white Steeds; with Wreaths his Chariot hung,
The Army follow'd with a joyfull song.

Lib. iv. od. ii. as by the Spectators also. *Horace,* of *Augustus,*

> *Tuque dum procedis,* Io TRIUMPHE,
> *Non semel dicemus,* Io TRIUMPHE.

Io TRIUMPHE whilst you march in state,
Io TRIUMPHE we reiterate.

Thus having briefly touched upon the Antiquity, and use of Triumphal Arches, we shall descend to the illustration of the Descriptions in particular.

THE

The firſt ARCH.

MUNDAY, *April* the two and twentieth, His MAJESTY went from the *Tower*, through the City, to *Whitehall*.

In his paſſage through *Crouched Fryers*, He was entertained with Muſick, a Band of eight Waits, placed on a Stage.

Near *Algate*, another Band of ſix Waits entertain'd him in like manner with Muſick, from a Balcony, built to that purpoſe.

In Leaden-Hall-Street, neer Lime-Street End, was erected the firſt Triumphal Arch, after the Dorick order. On the North-ſide, on a Pedeſtal before the Arch, was a Woman perſonating REBEL-LION, mounted on an Hydra, in a Crimſon Robe, torn, Snakes crawling on her Habit, and begirt with Serpents, her Hair ſnaky, a Crown of Fire on her Head, a bloody Sword in one Hand, a charming Rod in the other. Her Attendant CONFUSION, in a deformed Shape, a Garment of ſeverall ill-matched Colours, and put on the wrong way; on her Head, Ruines of Caſtles; torn Crowns, and broken Scepters in each Hand.

THere was no War in the *Roman*, or *Greek* Common-wealths call'd by any name properly anſwering to *Rebellion*, which comprehends only the violation of that Natural duty, which the Subject owes to the ſupreme Governour: for though we find *Rebellio* in *Tacitus*, of Subjects that riſe againſt their Prince, and *Rebellis* too in *Claudian*, ſpeaking of *Africk* a Subject to *Rome*, but then in Arms againſt the Roman Emperour under *Gildo*, as

> ——*ſegetes mirantur Iberas*
> *Horrea : nec Libyæ ſenſerunt damna rebellis*
> *Jam Tranſalpina contenti meſſe Quirites.*

In *Eutropium Lib.* 1.

> The Roman Grange *Iberian* Corn admires,
> Nor did rebellious *Libya's* loſs reſent,
> But with *Tranſalpine* Harveſts was content.

and in another place, ſpeaking of the *Moors*;

De bello Gildonico.

Nònne

Nónne meam fugiet Maurus, *cùm viderit, umbram?*
Quid dubitas? exsurge toris: invade rebellem :
Captivum mihi redde meum——

Will not the *Moor* fly when he sees my Ghoſt?
Why doubt'ſt Thou? riſe : ſtorm that Rebellious Coaſt;
My Captive me reſtore.——

Yet we find that word attributed alſo to *Alarick*, and his Army, no
Subjects of the *Roman* Empire, but only Confederates, by the ſame
Authour,

De V.I. Confolat. Honorii.
Oblatum Stilico *violato fœdere Martem*
Omnibus arripuit votis, ubi Roma peric'lo
Jam procul, & belli medius Padus *arbiter ibat :*
Jámque opportunam motu ſtrepuiſſe rebelli
Gaudes perfidiam.

He freely undertook ſo juſt a War,
The League being broke, and *Rome* from danger far,
While the Armies *Poe* divides; *Stilico* Arms :
Glad of th' occaſion thoſe Rebellious ſwarms
In ſuch a place conjoyn'd.

Wherefore we muſt look for its Deſcription under Civil Diſcord,
and Sedition, which *Petronius Arbiter*, in the Civil War betwixt *Cæ-
far* and *Pompey*, ha's very elegantly delivered.

Infremuere tubæ, ac ſciſſo DISCORDIA *crine*
Extulit ad Superos Stygium *caput. Hujus in ore*
Concretus ſanguis, contuſáque lumina flebant.
Stabant atrati ſcabrà rubigine dentes ;
Tabo lingua fluens ; obſeſſa draconibus ora :
Atque intertorto laceratam pectore veſtem,
Sanguineam tremulà quatiebat lampada dextrâ.

The Trumpets ſound, and Diſcord, with torn hair,
Her *Stygian* front advanceth to the air.

                                 O'rc

O're her ſmear'd Viſage clotted blood lies ſpread,
Her blubber'd Eyes are beat into her Head,
Her iron Teeth rough with a ruſty ſcale,
Her Tongue drops gore, Serpents her Brows impale :
Rending her pleited Veſt, and red Attire,
Her trembling Hand brandiſheth bloody Fire.

But we cannot better take a view of Sedition, and Diſcord, then in the Deſcription of the Authours of it, feign'd to be the Furies: as *Virgil*,

Tu potes unanimes armare in prælia fratres,
Atque odiis verſare domos : tu verbera teƈtis,
Funeréasque inferre faces : tibi nomina mille,
Mille nocendi artes : fœcundum concute peƈtus.
Disjice compoſitam pacem, ſere crimina belli :
Arma velit, poſcátque ſimul, rapiátque juventus.

Unanimous Brothers thou canſt arm to fight,
And ſettled Courts deſtroy with deadly ſpight :
Storm Palaces with Steel, and Pitchy Flames,
Thou haſt a thouſand wicked Arts, and Names :
Thy Boſom disembogue, with Miſchief full,
And Articles concluding Peace annull.
Then raiſe a War, and with bewitching Charms
Make the mad People rage to take up Arms.

Statius gives a Deſcription of one of them very correſpondent to ours,

Centum illi ſtantes umbrabant ora Ceraſtæ :   Thebaid.
Turba minor diri capitis ; Sedet intus abaƈtis   Lib. 1.
Ferrea lux oculis, qualis per nubila Phœbes
Atraciâ rubet arte labor : Suffuſa veneno
Tenditur, ac ſanie gliſcit cutis, igneus atro
Ore vapor, quo longa ſitis, morhíque, famésque,
Et populis mors una venit, riget horrida tergo
Palla, & cærulei redeunt in peƈtora nodi;

                                        Tum

Tum geminas quatit illa manus : hæc igne rogali
Fulminat, hæc vivo manus aëra verberat hydro.

An hundred Snakes up in a Party made
From her dire Head, her horrid Temples shade,
Her fix'd Eyes sunk, their Brazen Gleamings shroud,
So charm'd bright *Phœbe* blusheth through a Cloud:
Poyson'd her swoln Skin shines with gore, her Breath
Ushers in Flame, Thirst, Famine, Plague, and Death:
Her dreadful Robes rough on her Shoulders fit,
Which on her Bosom Crimson Ribbans knit:
Then both her hands she shakes; with Fun'ral Fire
This thunders, that jerks Air with Serpents dire.

Of *Tisiphone* Virgil,

Æn. vi.

Continuò sontes ultrix accincta flagello
Tisiphone quatit insultans, torvòsque sinistrà
Intentans angues, vocat agmina sæva sororum.

Cruel *Tisiphone* insulting shakes
Her dreadful Whip, and arm'd with twisted Snakes
In her left hand, straight on the guilty falls,
And Troops of unrelenting Furies calls.

Pindar calls Sedition ἐχθρὰν κυροτρόφον, *a bad Nurse for Children.* **The**
reason may be taken from these Verses of *Homer* describing the con-
sequents of it;

Iliad. xxii.

Ὑιὸς τ᾽ ἀπολυμένες, ἑλκυσθείσας τι θυγάτρας
Καὶ θαλάμες κεραϊζομένες, ἠ νήπια τέκνα
Βαλλόμενα ποτὶ γαίη; ὰ αἰνῆ δηϊοτῆ η,
Ἑλκομένας τε νυὸς ὀλοῆς ὑπὸ χερσὶν Ἀχαιῶν.

My slaughter'd Sons, my Daughters ravish'd, see,
My Court destroy'd, and from the Nurses knee
Their tender Babes snatch'd by the cruel Foe,
And in one Sea their Bloods commixed flow.

                                             The

The *HYDRA*, on which *Rebellion* is mounted, the Ancients have very variouſly repreſented. *Pauſanias* attributes but one Head to it, *Piſander Camirenſis* many, *Alcæus* nine, *Simonides* fiſty, ωυ'τσκ·ν'ξακἰρακ·ν, whom *Virgil* follows,

In Coriφ-thiatis. I Ibid.

> *Quinquaginta atris immanis hiatibus* Hydra
> *Savior intus habet ſedem* ——

Æn. vi.

> *Hydra* with fiſty ugly Jaws, one more
> Cruel then this by half,'s within the door.

" *On the* South Pedeſtal *is a Repreſentation of* BRITTAIN's MO-
" NARCHY, *ſupported by* LOYALTY, *both Women* ; Monarchy, *in a large*
" *Purple Robe, adorn'd with Diadems, and Scepters, over which a looſe*
" *Mantle, edg'd with blue and ſilver Fringe, reſembling Water, the*
" *Map of* Great Britain *drawn on it, on her Head* London, *in her*
" *right Hand,* Edinburgh ; *in her left,* Dublin : Loyalty *all in White,*
" *three Scepters in her right Hand, three Crowns in her left.*

Purple is call'd by *Tertullian Regiæ dignitatis inſigne, a Badg of Royal Dignity.* Lactantius, *Et ſicuti nunc* Romanis *indumentum Purpuræ inſigne eſt Regiæ dignitatis aſſumptæ, ſic illis,* &c. *Claudian of Ruſinus,*

De Idolol. Lib.iv.cap. vii. In Ruſinum, lib. ii.

> *Imperii certus ,tegeret ceu Purpura dudum*
> *Corpus, & ardentes ambirent tempora gemmæ.*

> Certain of Empire, as if Purple now
> Had cloath'd his Limbs, and Gems impal'd his Brow.

So *Strabo* ſays , that the Poſterity of *Androclus*, Son of *Codrus* King of *Athens*, had at *Epheſus*, beſides many other Honours granted them , *a Purple Robe in token of their Royal deſcent.* According to which, we finde in *Sidonius Apollinaris*, *Purpuratus* to be equivalent with *Imperator*, Epiſt. lib. ii. *Qui videbatur in jugulum Purpurati jamjam ruiturus* ; *Who ſeem'd ready to murder the Emperour* : and, *Serò cognoſcunt, poſſe reum Majeſtatis pronunciari etiam eum, qui non adſectaſſet habitum Purpuratarum*; *They too late underſtand, that even he, that affected not the Habit of the Emperours, might be found guilty of Treaſon.* From whence the *Civilians* obſerve, that it was Treaſon to aſſume the Royal Robes. And *Ammianus Marcellinus* ſpeaks of a Woman , who had ſuborn'd ſeveral to accuſe her Husband of High Treaſon, for having ſtoln the Emperour *Diocletian's* Purple Veſt out of his Sepulchre, and hiding it. *Euſebius* ;

Epiſt.xiii.

E   H 6

He (Diocletian) first beautified his Shoes with Gold, and Pearls, and preti-
ous Stones. For the Kings before him were honoured in the same manner
with the Confuls, having onely a *Purple Veft for a badge of their Royalty.*
The fame faith *Pæanius,* who tranflated *Eutropius ; The Royal Robe be-*
fore was diftinguifh'd only by its Purple colour. Wherefore, when any
refolv'd Tyrannically to fieze upon the Royal Dignity, they immediately ufurp'd a Purple Robe ; which they fometimes forc'd from a

In Claudi-
ano.

Standard, as *Trebellius* reports of *Saturninus.* The fame *Authour ;*
Gordianum *Proconfulem reclamantem, & fe terræ affligentem, opertum*
Purpura imperare coëgerunt & primò quidem invitus Gordianus *Purpuram*
fumpferat: poftea ve ò; quum vidit neque filio, neque familiæ id latam effe,
volens fufcepit Imperium ; They forc'd Gordian the Proconful, *who denied,*
and caft himfelf upon the ground, to be vefted in Purple, and receive the Title
of Emperour : *at firft he was very unwilling to receive the Purple Robe,*
but, when he faw, that that was unfafe for his Son, and Family, he receiv'd
the Empire willingly. Where *Purpuram fumere,* and *fumere Imperium,*
are the fame. Sometimes they committed Sacrilege upon the Statues

In Proculo
ibid.

of the Gods. Vopifcus ; *Depofità Purpurà ex fimulachro* Veneris,
cum cyclade uxoria à militibus circumftantibus amictus, & adoratus eft ;
Taking a Purple Robe from the Statue of Venus, *and his Wife's inner Veft of*
Gold, he was invefted, and adored by the Souldiers as Emperour, *Trebellius ;*
Celfum Imperatorem *appellaverunt peplo Deæ Cæleftis ornatum ; They*
put on Celfus *the Veft of the Goddefs of Heaven, and call'd him* Emperour.
Wherefore, when we read of the *Confular Purple Robes* under the *Ro-*
mane Emperours, as in that of *Latinus Pacatus, Quorum alter, poft am-*
pliffimos Magiftratus, & purpuras Confulares ; and of *Sidonius,*

_____ Te picta Togatum

Purpura plus capiat ; quia res eft femper ab ævo

Rara frequens Conful:_____

Purple fhould rather thee affect, fince we
One often made a *Conful* feldome fee :

it muft be underftood either of the *Senatorian* Segments added to their
Confular Robes, or of a *Purple* mix'd with fome other Dye ; which is
mentioned in *Theodofius's Code* : as a Warp of Purple, the Woof of another colour, or the like. For the *Imperial Interdict* comprehends all of
whatfoever degree ; *Temperent univerfi, cujuscunque fint fexus, digni-*
tatis, artis, profeffionis, & generis, ab hujusmodi fpeciei poffeffione,
quæ foli Principi, ejusque domui dedicatur ; Let every one, of what Sex,
Dignity, Art, Profeffion, and Birth they be, forbear the poffeffion of this
fort of Purple, which is appropriated to the Prince alone, and his houfe.
The

The first Imperial Edict of this nature is conceived to be in the time of the Emperour *Nero*: which is to be understood *de holoveris*, of pure unmix'd Purple.

Neither was Purple peculiar to the Imperial Robes onely, but to their Pens too. The Emperour *Leo* forbad, that any Rescripts of his should bear other then a Purple Inscription. So *Nicetas*, in the Life of *Manuel* the Emperour, says, That, at his entrance upon the Empire, he sent Letters to *Constantinople*, written with Purple. *Constantinus Manasses* in his Annals, *The Emperour granted the request of his Sister, and taking a Pen in his hand confirm'd the Paper in Purple Letters*, And *Palæologus* the Emperour, swearing subjection to the *Roman* See in the Church of *Santo Spirito* at *Rome*, subscribed in Letters of Purple.

The art of making this Purple, both for Robes, and Ink, is still preserv'd, but we meet not with the materials; though we have left us both the place, and manner of taking, preparing, and whatsoever is necessary for that purpose.

Monarchy is said to be supported by *Loyalty*; because the Love of the Subject is the securest Guard of the Prince. *Seneca*, in a Discourse betwixt *Nero* and *Seneca* the Philosopher,

> NE. *Ferrum tuetur Principem.* SE. *Meliùs Fides.*
> NE. *Decet timeri Cæsarem.* SE. *At plùs diligi.*

> NE. Arms *Cæsar* guard. SE. But better Loyalty.
> NE. Kings should be fear'd. SE. They rather lov'd should be.

We find not any name for *Loyalty* in the time of the *Roman* Emperours, except *Fides*, or *Fidelitas* : as in the Coyns of the Emperour *Philippus*,

which was signified by the extension of the hand· *Lucan* speaking of the Army, promising Fealty to *Julius Cæsar*,

— — His cunctis simul assensere cohortes,
Elatásque altè, quæcunque ad bella vocaret,
Promisere manus — — —

All rais'd their hands with joint consent, that they
Would fight for him, and his Commands obey
'Gainst whomsoe're — — —

Isidorus Hispal. *Mos erat Militaris, ut, quoties consentiret exercitus, quia voce non potest, manu promittat :* It was the Military Custom, that as often as the Army consented, because they could not with their voice, they should promise with their hand.

Which Posture is represented in these *Medaigles* of the Emperours *Trajan*, and *Hadrian*,

Oyselet.
Tab. xxxiii.
& xxxvii.

Claudian, speaking of a Rebellion in the *Western* parts of the Empire,

Interea turbata FIDES, civilia rursus
Bella tonant, dubiumque quatit Discordia mundum.

Mean while the Peace was broke, Ensigns unfurl'd,
And Discord thundring shook the stagg'ring World.

Loyalty is cloathed in white, to signifie its purity, and innocency. *Color albus præcipuè decorus Deo est, tum in cæteris, tum maximè in textili,* Cicero. *Horace.*

Lib. 1. Od.
XXXV.

Te Spes, & albo rara Fides colit
Velata panno — — —
Thee Hope, and Faith embrace
Cloathed in white.

                                         " The

" *The firſt Painting on the South-ſide is a Proſpect of His Majeſtie's*
" *landing at Dover-Caſtle, Ships at Sea, great Guns going off, one kneeling,*
" *and kiſsing the King's Hand, Souldiers, Horſe, and Foot, and many*
" *People gazing : above,*

ADVENTUS AUG:

" *Beneath the Painting this Motto,*

IN SOLIDO RURSUS FORTUNA LOCAVIT,

This Inſcription ADVENTUS AUGUSTI is often found among the
Coyns of the *Roman* Emperours upon a peaceable return ; which is
ſignified by the extenſion of the right hand : for ſaith *Quintilian, Fit &*
ille habitus, qui eſſe in Statuis Pacificator ſolet, qui protenſo brachio manum
inflexo pollice extendit ; That Geſture is uſed too , which in Statues is a token
of Peace, which extends the Arm, and Hand, inflecting the Thumb. In which
Poſture there is extant at *Rome* the Statue of the Emperour *M. Aure-*
lius Antoninus : and another before the *Laterane,* mention'd in the Addi-
tions to *Pierius.* Theſame we finde in the Coyns of *M. Julius Philippus,*
and *Fl. Jovianus,* with the ſame Inſcription, ADVENTUS AUGUSTI.

Inſtitut. Lib.
XI. cap. iii.

Cuſper.
Tat. viii.
Roma. Tom.
iv. Annal.

" *The Painting on the North-ſide, oppoſite to this, is a Trophy with decol-*
" *lated Heads, having over it,*

ULTOR A TERGO DEUS.

" *Taken out of* Horace ;

——— *ſequitur Rebelles*

Ultor à tergo Deus ———

" *God's Vengeance Rebels at the Heels purſues.*

The Motto beneath,

AUSI IMMANE NEFAS, AUSOQUE POTITI.

A

A Trophy amongst the ancient *Romans* was ordinarily a Trunk of a Tree, fitted with the Arms of the Conquered Enemy, according to that of *Virgil*,

Æn. Lib. xi.

> *Ingentem quercum, decisis undique ramis,*
> *Constituit tumulo, fulgentiáque induit arma,*
> *Mezenti Ducis exuvias, tibi magne tropæum*
> *Bellipotens : aptat rorantes sanguine cristas,*
> *Teláque trunca viri, & his sex thoraca petitum*
> *Perfossúmque locis, clypeúmque ex ære sinistræ*
> *Subligat, atque ensem collo suspendit eburnum.*

> A stately Oak on Rising-Ground he plac'd,
> And Boughs disrob'd, with glorious Armour grac'd ;
> With King *Mezentius* Spoils the Trunks he loads,
> Great *Mars*, thy Trophy, Warlik'st of the Gods ;
> His Breast-Plate, run twice six times thorow, rears,
> And Plumes bedew'd with Blood, and broken Spears,
> His Brazen Shield on the left Shoulder tied,
> Hanging his Sword in Ivory by th'side.

And in the same Book,

> *Da nunc, Tybri pater, ferro, quod missile libro,*
> *Fortunam, atque viam duri per pectus Halesi,*
> *Hæc arma, exuviásque viri tua quercus habebit.*

> Grant, Father *Tyber*, Fortune to this Lance,
> And that this Jav'lin, which I now advance,
> May through *Halesus* Bosom passage make,
> And let thy Oak his Spoils, and Armour take.

Statius,

Thebaid. Lib. ii.

> *Quercus erat, teneræ jamdudum oblita juventæ,*
> *Huic laves galeas, perfossáque vulnere crebro*

Inserit

Inferit arma ferens, huic truncos ictibus enfes
Subligat, & fractas membris spirantibus haftas.

There was an aged Oak, on which he put
Bruis'd Casks, and Corflets, thruft-through, hack'd, and cut:
Next Swords in Battel broken guirds upon,
And fplinter'd Spears from dying Bodies drawn.

The Trophie of *Jupiter* over the Giants is at large, and elegantly
defcribed by *Claudian*,

————Phlegræis *fylva fuperbit*
Exuviis, totùmque nemus victoria veftit.
Hic patuli rictus, hic prodigiofa Gigantum
Tergora dependent, & adhuc crudele minantur
Affixæ facies truncis : immaniàque offa
Serpentum paffim tumulis exfanguibus albent,
Et rigidæ multo fufpirant fulmine pelles,
Nullàque non magni jactat fe nominis arbor.
Hæc centum-gemini ftrictos Ægeonis enfes
Curvatâ vix fronde levat ; liventibus illa
Exultat Cori fpoliis : hæc arma Mimantis
Suftinet; hos onerat ramos exutus Ophion.
Altior & cunctis abies, umbrofàque latè,
Ipfius Enceladi fumantia geftat opima
Summi Terrigenùm regis, caderétque gravatâ
Pondere, nì lapfum fulciret proxima quercus.
Indè timor, numénque loco, nemorísque fenectæ
Parcitur, æthereísque nefas nocuiffe Tropæis.

De raptu Profeip. Lib. iii.

———— The Woods in Spoils *Phlegræan* pride,
The whole Grove Vict'ry cloath'd. Here Gapings wide
Of horrid Jaws ; there Backs of hideous fize
Hung, and ftak'd faces threatning ftill the Skies:

Huge

Huge Serpents Skeletons in bloodless Piles
There bleaching white lay in voluminous Coyls,
Whose scaly Sloughs smell with Sulphureous Flame :
No Tree but boasts some mighty Giant's Name.
This, loaden, under stern *Ægæon* yields,
Who us'd an hundred Swords, as many Shields;
That brags bold *Corus* bloody Spoils: this bears
The Arms of *Mimas*; that *Ophion's* wears.
But higher then the rest, with spreading shade,
A Firr *Enceladus* Crest and Corslet lade,
The Giants King; which with its weight had broke,
If not supported by a neighb'ring Oak.
Hence a Religious Aw preserves the Woods,
And none dares wrong the Trophies of the Gods.

Lib. iii.
cap. ii.

But when the City of *Rome* grew greater in power, the Trophies were more magnificent. L. Florus, *How acceptable those two Victories were, may be conjectured from hence, that* Domitius Ahenobarbus, *and* Fabius Maximus *erected in the same place where the Battels were fought Turrets of Stone, upon which were Trophies, adorn'd with the Arms of the Enemy, a Custome not in use before amongst us. For the people of* Rome *never upbraided their Conquered Enemies with their Victories.*

Lib. ii.

On these Trophies was inscribed both the Name of the Conquerour, and the People conquered. Tacitus, *Laudatis pro concione victoribus,* Cæsar *congeriem armorum struxit superbo cum titulo ; debellatis inter* Rhenum Albimque *nationibus, exercitum* Tiberii Cæsaris *ea Monimenta* Marti, & Jovi, & Augusto *sacravisse :* Cæsar, *having commended the Victors, raised an heap of Arms with this proud Inscription, The Army of* Tiberius Cæsar, *having vanquish'd the People between the River* Rhene, *and the* Albe, *consecrates these Monuments to* Mars, Jupiter, *and* Augustus. And, to the same purpose, *Miles in loco prælii* Tiberium *Imperatorem salutavit* (absentem) *struxitque aggerem, & in modum Tropæorum arma, subscriptis victarum gentium nominibus, imposuit.* There are two Trophies of *Marius's* still remaining at *Rome*, one of which ha's a Breast-Plate with Military Ornaments, and Shields, before it a young man captive, with his hands bound behind him; on each side of it two Winged Victories. So *Pliny* tells us of a Trophie erected to the honour

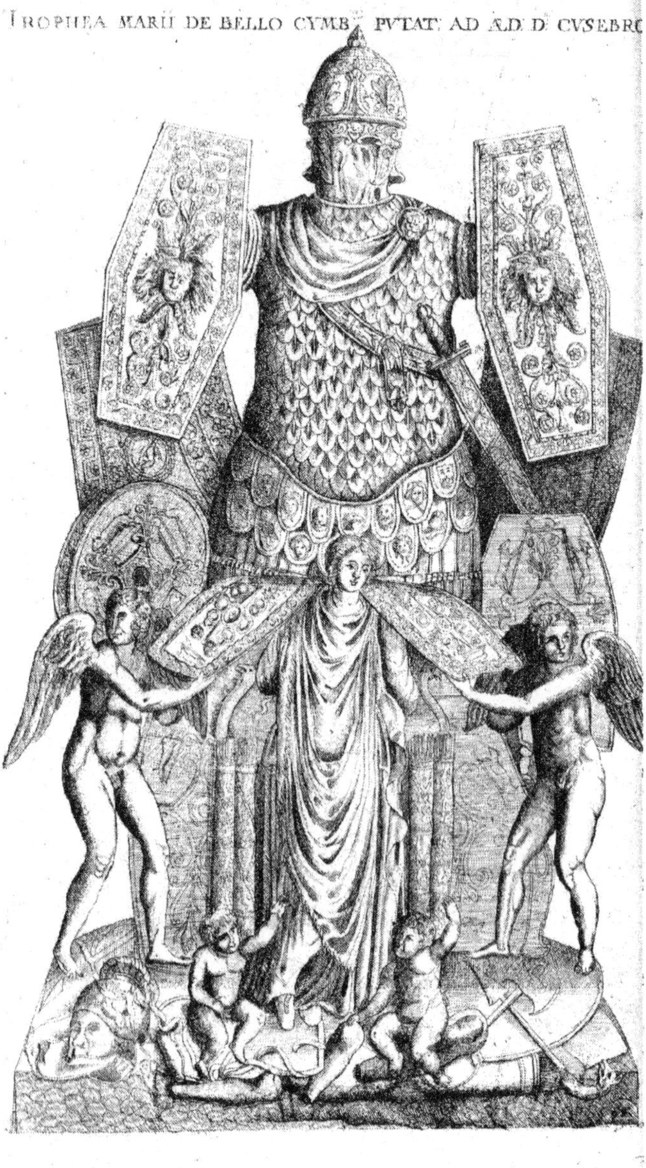
TROPHEA MARII DE BELLO CYMB. PVTAT. AD ÆD. D. CVSEBR

PHÆA MARII DE BELLO CIMBR: PVTAT. AD ÆD. D. EVSEBIVM ROMÆ.

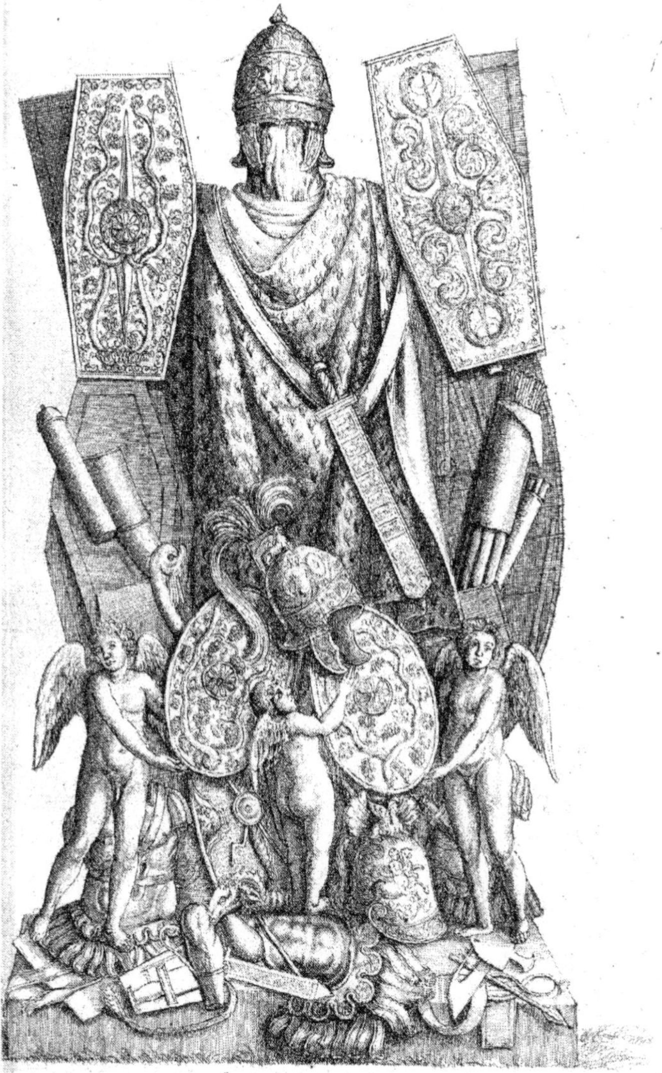

nour of *Augustus* in the *Alps* with this Inscription; IMPERATORI CÆSARI
DIVI F. AUG. PONTIF. MAX. IMPERATORI XIV. TRIBUNITIÆ
POTESTATIS. S. P. Q. R. QUOD EIUS DUCTU AUSPICIISQVE
GENTES ALPIUM OMNES, QVÆ A MARI SUPERO AD INFIMUM
PERTINEBANT, SUB IMPERIUM P. R. SUNT REDACTÆ. *Stobæus*
says, that *Othryades*, taking the Spoils of some of his Enemies, erected
a Trophy, and writ this Title with the Blood of the wounded, *Nat. Hist. Lib. iii. cap. xx.* *Tit. De Fortitis.*

THE LACEDÆMONIANS OVER THE ARGIVES.

These Trophies were consecrated to the Gods, and therefore could
not be demolish'd without Sacrilege. So *Dio* says of *Cæsar*, that, after *Lib. xli*
his *Pontick* Victory, he durst not deface the Trophy of *Mithridates*,
ὡς ῇ τῶ ἐναλλίῳ Θεῶ ἱερωμ, because *sacred to the Gods of War.* So, when
his Friends had given order, that a Sword, which hung up in a Temple of the *Arubeni*, as a Spoil from *Cæsar*, should be taken down,
ὡς ἱερον, ὡδ᾽ εγκωρ, he would not suffer it, accounting it sacred. Vitruvius, *Lib. ii.*
Postea autem Rhodii, *religione impediti, quòd nefas esset Tropæa dicata re-
movere, circa locum eum ædificium struxerunt;* But afterwards the Rho-
dians, out of a religious fear, because it was unlawful to remove the dedicated
Trophies, erected a Building about the place. The Gods, to whom the Ro- *Lib. xiv.*
mans consecrated their Trophies, we finde in *Livy : Omnis generis arma*
cumulata in ingentem acervum, precatus Martem, Minervâmque, Luûm-
que Matrem, & *cæteros Deos, quibus spolia dicare jus fasque est.*

The Motto ULTOR A TERGO DEUS, over the
Trophie, is in reference to the Coyn of the Emperour *Claudius,* which
represents *Martem Ultorem* with a *Trophie* on his Shoulder,

but more particularly to that History of *Augustus,* who, after the War
was ended, which he undertook for the revenge of his Father's blood,
murdered

Dio, lib.liv
Suetonius. murdered by some *Common-wealth's* men in the *Senate*-house, consecrated a Temple *MARTI ULTORI*, which he had vowed during the War. *Ovid,*

Faft. Lib.v.
> Mars ades, & satia scelerato sanguine ferrum,
> Steíque Favor causa pro meliore tuis :
> Templa feres ; &, me Victore, vocaberis ULTOR.
> Voverat, & fuso lætus ab hoste redit.

> Glut Steel, O *Mars*, with impious Blood ; incline
> To my just Cause, a Temple shall be thine :
> I Conqu'rour, Thou shalt be *REVENGER* stil'd.
> He vow'd, and glad return'd, his Enemy foil'd.

The Form of the *TEMPLE* we have in this Coyn of *Augustus,*

Occal. Pag.
225.

Faft.ibid. So when he had re-taken the Colours from the *Parthians,* which *Crassus* had lost, he gave him the Title of *BIS-ULTOR. Ovid,*

> Rité Deo Templiámque datum, noménque BIS-ULTOR,
> Emeritus voti debita solvit honor.

> The God BIS-ULTOR stil'd, his Temple made,
> So he his Vows devoutly paid.

We

We finde alſo mention of *MARS ULTOR* in an ancient Inſcription in *Gruter*. Pag. cccxvii. 8.

D.　　M.
T. FLAVIO. AUG. LIB.
LIBERALI. ÆDITUO
MARTIS. ULTORIS
CLAUDIA. EX OCHE
CONJUGI
BENEMERENTI. ET.
SIBI. FECIT.
VIXIT. ANN. LVII.

The *Motto* beneath the *Trophy* is taken out of *Virgil*, who ſpoke it of thoſe, who were, for the like Crimes, condemn'd to the Pains of *Erebus*, as he cloſes the Deſcription of it in the Sixth of his *Æneis*,

Hic quibus inviſi fratres, dum vita manebat,
Pulſatiſve parens, & fraus innexa clienti ;
Aut qui divitiis ſoli incubuère repertis,
Nec partem poſuère ſuis ; (quæ maxima turba eſt ;)
Quique ob adulterium cæſi, quique arma ſequuti
Impia, nec veriti dominorum fallere dextras ;
Incluſi pœnam expectant : nè quære doceri,
Quam pœnam ; aut quæ forma viros, fortunáve merſit.
Saxum ingens volvunt alii, radiiſque rotarum
Diſtricti pendent : ſedet, æternúmque ſedebit
Infelix Theſeus : Phlegyáſque miſerrimus omnes
Admonet, & magnà teſtatur voce per umbras,
"Diſcite juſtitiam moniti, & non temnere Divos.
Vendidit hic auro patriam, dominúmque potentem
Impoſuit ; fixit leges pretio, atque refixit ;
Hic thalamum invaſit natæ, vetitóſque Hymenæos :
Auſi omnes immane nefas, auſóque potiti.

F 2　　　　　　　　Here

Here Brother-haters are with Pains repai'd,
Who slew their Parents, or their Friends betrai'd ;
Or brooding lay on Golden Heaps alone,
These thousands are, which did impart to none ;
Those in Adult'ry slain ; or those rebel,
And did their native Prince to Traitors sell,
Here meet their Dooms ; seek not these Woes to sound,
Nor by what way Fate did their Souls confound :
These rowl huge Stones, and stretch'd on Wheels do lie ;
There *Theseus* sits, and shall eternally ;
Aloud, through Shades, sad *Phlegyas* mourning cries,
Admonish'd, Justice learn, nor Gods despise.
This to a potent Prince his Country sold,
And Laws enacted, and repeal'd for Gold ;
That beds his Daughter, and no Incest spar'd :
All dar'd bold Crimes, and thriv'd in what they dar'd.

" *The Painting over the Middle Arch represents the* King, *mounted in*
" *calm Motion,* USURPATION *flying before him, a Figure*
" *with many ill-favoured Heads, some bigger, some lesser, and one parti-*
" *cularly shooting out of his Shoulder, like* CROMWEL'S ;
" *Another Head upon his Rump, or Tayl ; Two Harpies with a Crown,*
" *chased by an Angel ; Hell's Jaws opening. Under the said Represen-*
" *tation of the King ; is sung Usurpation is this Motto,*

VOLVENDA DIES EN ATTULIT ULTRO,

" *Taken out of the Ninth Book of the* Æneis,

Turne, quod optanti Divûm promittere nemo
Auderet, volvenda dies, en ! attulit ultró.

" What none of all the Gods durst grant, implor'd,
" Successive Time does of its own accord.

The *Harpies* were described by the Ancients with the Faces of Virgins. *Hesiod,*

'Ἁρπυίας

Ἡράκλεε ῷ Ἀρπυίας, Ἀελλώ τ᾽, Ὠκυπέτην τε,
Ἀι ῥ᾽ ἀνέμων πνοιῇσι, ἠ διωτοῖς ἅμ᾽ ἑκάντεν,
Ὠκείης πτερύγεσσι.

In Theogo-
nia.

Aello, and *Ocupet*, *Harpyes*, who,
Fair hair'd, the Winds, and nimble Birds purſue,
Born on ſwift Wings.———

and *Virgil*,

Æneid iii.

See *Rhodigi-
nus*, lib. xvi.
cap. xxvi.

——————*Quas dira* Celæno,
Harpyiæque *colunt aliæ,* Phineia *poſtquàm*
Clauſa domus, menſaſque metu iquére priores.
Triſtius haud illis monſtrum, nec ſævior ulla
Peſtis, & ira Deûm, Stygiis *ſeſe extulit undis.*
Virginei volucrum vultus, fœdiſsima ventris
Proluvies, uncæque manus, & pallida ſemper
Ora fame.

Where dire *Celæno* other *Harpyies* led,
When frighted they from *Phineas* Table fled.
No Monſter like to theſe, no Plague more fell,
Nor ſharper Vengeance Heav'n e're call'd from Hell.
The Fowl have Virgin Faces, and hook'd Claws,
Still purging Bellies, always greedy Maws,
With Hunger pale.———

The Form of theſe *Harpyies* is to be ſeen in Sculpture in the Church
of Saint *Martin* at *Venice,* frequented, as a *Maſter-Piece* to draw theſe
Monſters by, both by *Carvers,* and *Painters;* ſays *Erythræus* on this
place of *Virgil.* They were expreſſed alſo with crooked Claws, from
whence they were called ————

Apollonius,

Ἀλλὰ διὰ νεφέων ἅψα ————
Ἀρπυίαι ψιλαι ῷ χειρὶ τὸ τὸ————
Σκαιοῖσι, ὑπαλξι. ————

Argonaut.
lib. ii.

Biit

But *Harpyies*, hurried swiftly through the Air,
From Mouth, and Hands, with griping Talons tear
Still all away. ———————

Rutilius Numantianus, in his *Itinerary*,

Harpyiæ, *quarum discerpitur unguibus Orbis*,
Quæ pede glutineo quæ tetigére trahunt.

Harpyies, who rend the World, whose Bird-lime Feet,
And Talons, bear away whate're they meet.

There is a Coyn yet extant of *L. Valerius*, where we have an *Harpye* thus represented,

That they had Wings, we finde in *Æschylus*, who, mentioning the *Furies* asleep about *Orestes*, doubting what they should be, says, they could not be *Harpyies* (for he had seen them often painted robbing *Phineus*'s Table) because they had no Wings.

" *Above the Arch, on two Pedestals, South-ward, and North-ward,*
" *stand the Statues of* King James, *and* King Charles *the*
" *First. In the middle somewhat higher, just over the Arch, the Statue of*
" *His Sacred Majesty. Under that of* King James,

DIVO JACOBO.

" *Under that of* King Charles *the First,*

DIVO CAROLO.

"*Under*

" Under that of His Majeſty this following Inſcription,

D. N.

CAROLO II.

D. G. BRITANNIARUM IMP.

OPT. MAX.

UBIQVE VENERANDO,

SEMPER AUG.

BEATISSIMO AC PIISSIMO,

BONO REIP. NATO,

DE AVITA BRITANNIA,

DE OMNIUM HOMINUM GENERE

MERITISSIMO,

P. P.

EXTINCTORI TYRANNIDIS,

RESTITUTORI LIBERTATIS,

FUNDATORI QUIETIS,

OB FELICEM REDITUM;

EX VOTO L. M.

P.

S. P. Q. L.

The

The Title of *DIVUS* was conftantly attributed by the *Romans* to their *Emperours* after their Confecration, or *Apotheosis*. *Ovid*, of *Julius Cæsar*,

> *Hanc animam intereà, cæso de corpore raptam,*
> *Fac jubar, ut semper Capitolia nostra, Forùmque,*
> *Divus ab excelsà prospectet Julius æde.*

> Mean while from his flain Corps his Soul convay
> Up to the Stars, and give it a clear Ray :
> That he, now *DIVUS*, may with influence
> Shine on our *Capitol*, and *Court* from thence.

Ælius Spartianus ; Hadrianus, *rogante* Antonino, *DIVUS à Senatu appellatus est :* Hadrian, *at the request of* Antoninus *his Succeffour, had the Title of* Divus *granted him by the Senate.* So *Claudian* feigns the Emperour *Theodofius* to affume that Title immediately upon his death,

> ———— *Cùm* Divus *abirem,*
> *Res incompofitas, fateor, tumidásque reliqui.*

> When I a God went hence, I left, 'tis true,
> The bufnefs hard, and much unfettled too.

After which *Confecration* they had *Temples* dedicated to them, (which *Auguftus* admitted, while he was yet alive) *Flamens*, and *Under-Priefts*. Seneca of *Auguftus*,

In Octavia.

> *Pietate gnati factus eximià Deus,*
> *Post fata confecratus, & Templis datus.*

> Made by his Son's great Piety a God,
> Temples he built for him, and Altars had.

Ibid.

> *Sic ille patriæ primus* Auguftus *parens*
> *Complexus aftra eft, colitur & Templis Deus.*

> Thus the firft Father of his Countrey had
> In Heav'n a place, and worfhip'd as a God.

Spartian,

Spartian, *Qui Templum ei pro Sepulchro apud* Puteolos *conſtituit , &*
Quinquennale certamen, & Flamen, *&* Sodales, *& multa alia, quæ ad ho-*
norem quaſi Numinis pertinerent. *The Senate erected him* (Hadrian) *a*
Temple for a Sepulchre at Puzzolo, *with a Quinquennial Game, a* Flamen,
and Sodales, *and many other things belonging to the Honour of a God.* The
Flamen, and *Sodales* of the deceaſed *Emperour,* we often meet with in ancient Inſcriptions, as of *Cæſar's Flamen,*

M. PUBLICIO

M.F. SAB. SEXTIO
CALPURNIANO
EQVO. PUBLICO
FLAM. DIVI. JULI
PRÆF. ÆDIL. POT
QUÆSTOR. ÆRAR
SACERD.JUVEN.BRIX
COLLEGIA
CENTON. ET. FABROR.

and of *Hadrian's Sodales,*

L. FABIO. M. F. GAL. CILONI
SEPTIMINO. COS. PRAEF. URB
LEGG. AUGG. PR. PR. PANNON
SUPER DUCI. VEXILL. LEG. PRO
PR. PROVINCIAR. MOESIAE SUPER
PONTI ET BITHYNIÆ
COMITI. AUG. LEG. AUGG. PRO
PR. PROV. GALATIAE PRAEF.
AER. MILITARIS. PROV.
COS. ITEM. Q. LEG. PROV. NARBONENS
LEG. LEG. XVI. EL. F. SAMOSATE
SODAL. HADRIANAL
PR. URB. TRIB. PL. EB. Q. PROV
CRETAE. TRIB. LEG. XI. CL.
X. VIR STLITIB. JUDICANDIS
MEDIOLANENSIS
PATRONO.

G   The

The manner, and folemnity of their *Confecrations* is at large delivered
by *Herodian*. There was a four-fquare Pile built of feveral Stories,
fill'd with combuftible matter ; in the fecond was laid the Body of the
deceafed Emperour : in the *uppermoft, and leaft of the Stories was held
an Eagle.* As foon as the Pile was fet on fire, the Eagle was let fly : which
the Romans *think carries the Emperour's Soul from Earth to Heaven.
From which time he is worfhip'd with the reft of the Gods.* The Form of
the *Funeral Pile*, and the manner of their Tranflation into Heaven,
we finde in many Coyns of the *Emperours* : as in thefe of *Antoninus
Pius*, and *L. Verus*,

† lib. iv.

Claudian ha's prefumed to tell us the way they went thither, fpeaking
of the Death of THEODOSIUS,

De iii. Con-fulatu Hono-rii.

<blockquote>

————— *nec plura loquutus,*

Sicut erat, liquido fignavit tramite nubes,

Ingrediturque globum Lunæ, luménque reliquit

Arcadis, *& Veneris clementes pervolat auras. .*

Hinc Phœbi *permenfus iter, flammámque nocentem*

Gradivi, *placidúmque Jovem, ftetit arce fupremâ,*

Algenti quo zona riget Saturnia *tractu.*

Machina laxatur cœli, rutilæque patefcunt

Sponte fores. Arctôa *parat convexa* Boôtes.

Auftrales *referat portas fuccinctus* Orion,

Invitântque novum fidus, pendéntque viciffim,

Quas partes velit ille fequi, quibus effe fodalis

Dignetur ftellis, aut quâ regione moveri.

</blockquote>

nor

    ——— nor more he said;
But through the yielding Clouds his passage made,
And reach'd the *Moon*, then *Mercury* forsakes,
And to the milder Sphere of *Venus* makes :
Thence to the *Sun*, and *Mars* malignant fire,
And milder *Jove*; then mounts the highest Sphere,
Where in a colder Circle *Saturn* lords.
Heaven's Purple Gates ope of their own accords.
Him to his *Northern* Car *Boötes* courts,
Orion girt unlocks the *Southern* Ports,
And the new Star invite : both him intreat
He would vouchsafe to nominate his Seat ;
What Stars for his Associates he approv'd,
And in which Constellation would be mov'd.

 They questioned not the *Attributes* even of the worst of their *Emperours* ; as we see in these Verses of *Lucan* on *Nero*, that Prodigie of Nature,

   ——— *Te, cùm, statione peractâ,*
Astra petes serus, prælati regia cœli
Excipiet gaudente polo : seu sceptra tenere,
Seu te flammiferos Phœbi *transcendere currus,*
Tellurémque, nihil mutato Sole *timentem,*
Igne vago lustrare juvat : tibi Numine *ab omni*
Cedetur, jurique tuo Natura *relinquet,*
Quis Deus esse velis, ubi regnum ponere mundi.
Sed neque in Arctos *sedem tibi legeris orbe ;*
Nec *polus adversi ca'idus quà vergitur* Austri,
Unde tuam videas obliquo sidere Romam.
Ætheris immensi partem si presseris unam,
Sentiet axis onus : librati pondera cœli
Orbe tene medio: pars ætheris illa sereni
Tota vacet, nullæque obstent à Cæsare *nubes.*

     G 2   —— Thee

—— Thee, ah ! when, late, thou us shalt leave,
Courts pav'd with Stars shall joyfully receive,
Inviting thee to govern, or to sway
In *Phœbus* Chariot, and command the day :
Earth will not fear to see a newer Sun
With brighter Raies through th'old Eclipticks run.
Thee those, whom Heav'n's Apartiments enclose,
And Nature leaves unto thy own *dispose*,
To be what God thou wilt, and where to raign :
But not thy Palace near the *Northern* Wain ;
Nor *Southern* Stars intemperate Heat, erect,
Rome to behold with an oblique Aspect :
Sit in the middle, left the Pole should crack
Under thy weight ; poise the bright Zodiack,
Clear a Celestial House, where never Cloud
Shall *Cæsar*'s Star with duskie Vapours shroud.

We finde like expressions to those in the Inscription under His present Majesty, in several of the old ones collected by *Gruter* ; as *Page* CLII. 8.

DN, GLORIOSISS. ADQ. IN

CLUTUS. REX. THEODORICUS. VICT.
AC. TRIF. SEMPER. AUG. BONO REIP.
NATUS. CUSTOS. LIBERTATIS. ET
PROPAGATOR. ROMANI. NOMINIS.
DOMITOR. GENTIUM.

And *Page* CCXLVII. 3.

IMP. CAES. NER. TRAIANO
AUG. GERM. DAC. PARTH. PON
MAX. TR. P. XV. COS. VI. P. P. DE
ROM. IMPERIO. DE. PATERNA
ET. AVITA. HISP. PATRIA. ET. DE
OMNI. HOMIN. GEN. MERITISS
POPULARES. PROVINC
AREVATUM
OPTIMO. PRINC.   Behind

" *Behind the ſaid Figure of* CHARLES *the Second, in a large Table*
" *is deciphered the* ROYAL OAK *bearing Gowns, and Scepters,*
" *inſtead of Acorns; amongſt the Leaves, in a Label,*

MIRATURQVE NOVAS FRONDES ET NON SUA POMA.

——————— " *Leaves unknown*
" *Admiring, and ſtrange Apples not her Own.*

" *As deſigning its Reward for the Shelter afforded His Majeſty after the*
" *Fight at* Worceſter : *an expreſsion of* Virgil's *, ſpeaking of the*
" *Advancement of Fruits by the Art of Graffing.*

" *The upper Paintings on the* Eaſt-ſide *are Ruinous , repreſenting the*
" *Diſorder the Kingdom was in, during His Majeſtie's Abſence ; with*
" *this Motto,*

EN QVO DISCORDIA CIVES!

" *But on the* Weſt-ſide *they are finiſhed, to repreſent the Reſtauration*
" *of our Happineſs by His Majeſtie's Arrival ; the Motto,*

FELIX TEMPORUM REPARATIO.

" *On the* Royal Oak *in a Label,*

ROBUR BRITANNICUM.

In alluſion to His Majeſtie's Royal *Navy,* thoſe Floating Garri-
ſons made of Oak. For *Themiſtocles* ha's obſerv'd, that ' *Whoſoever de-* [margin: ¹ Tull. ad Attic. Lib. i. Ep. 13.]
ſires a ſecure Dominion by Land, muſt firſt get the Dominion of the Sea. And
therefore, when the *Oracle,* in the *Median* War, wiſh'd the *Athenians*
to provide a *Wall of Wood* for their Defence , he ᵐ interpreted it a [margin: ᵐ Plutarch. In vita Themiſtocle, and De vitando are alien.]
Navy.

" *Over the* Great Table,

REDEUNT SATURNIA REGNA.

Which are at large deſcribed by ¹ *Ovid,* [margin: ¹ Metam Lib. i.]

Aurea prima ſata eſt ætas ; quæ, vindice nullo,
Sponte ſuà , ſine lege, fidem, rectùmque colebat, &c.

The

The Golden Age *was first ; which, uncompel'd,*
And without rule, in Faith, and Truth excel'd.
As then, there was nor Punishment, nor Fear,
Nor threatning Laws in Brass prescribed were.
Nor suppliant crouching Pris'ners shook to see
Their angry Judge : but all was safe, and free.
To visit other Worlds no wounded Pine
Did yet from Hills to faithless Seas decline.
Then unambitious Mortals knew no more,
But their own Countrie's Nature-bounded Shore.
Nor Swords, nor Arms were yet : no Trenches round
Besieged Towns, nor strifeful Trumpet's sound.
The Souldier of no use. In firm content,
And harmless ease, their happy days were spent.
The yet-free Earth did of her own accord
(Untorn with Ploughs) all sorts of Fruit afford.
'Twas always Spring : warm Zephyrus *sweetly blew*
On smiling Flowers, which without setting grew.
Forthwith the Earth Corn, unmanured, bears ;
And ev'ry year renews her Golden Ears.
With Milk, and Nectar, were the Rivers fill'd,
And Honey from green Holly-Oaks distill'd.

Mr. SANDYS.

" *Under King* CHARLES *the Second,*

RESTITUTOR URBIS,

" *The Painting on the South-west side represents the Lord Mayor ; deli-*
" *vering to the King the Keys of the City.*
" *In the Niches are four Figures. The first on the South-side, a Woman*
" *in pleasant Colours ; the Emblem on her Shield, a Terrestrial Globe ;*
" *the Sun rising, Bats, and Owls flying to the Shadow : the Word,*

EXCOECAT CANDOR.

"The

" *The Second hath on her Escutcheon a Swarm of Bees, whetting their*
" *Stings : the Word,*

PRO REGE EXACUUNT.

Pliny ha's observed, that of Animals none , but a Bee, ha's a *King.*
Their Loyalty to him he ha's at large described.   *The Obedience of*   *Nat. Hist.*
the Communalty is to be admired. Whensoever the KING *goes* lib. xi. cap.
forth , the whole Hive accompanie him, gather round about him, encom- xvii.
pass him, protect him, and suffer him not to be seen. Whensoever the Com-
munalty is at work , he oversees them, and is alone free from the labour.
About him there is constantly a certain Guard, the daily preservers of his
authority. When they go forth, every one desires to be next the King, and
rejoyces to be seen in his duty. When he is weary , they ease him with their
shoulders : when he is altogether tired, they carry him.

Claudian says, that they reverence their *Prince* at his Birth ;

———— *sic mollibus olim*
Stridula ducturum pratis examina Regem
Nascentem venerantur apes. ———

So for their new-born King the Bees take Arms,
Who's through the Meads to lead their humming swarms.

From whence the *Ægyptians* made a B E E the *Hieroglyphick* of a
Loyal People.

" *The Third, on the* North *side, hath on her Shield a Mountain burn-*
" *ing,* Cities, *and* Vine-yards *destroyed, and ruined : the Word,*

IMPIA FOEDERA.

The Covenant : in abhorrence of which villainous Combination,
according to this Order of both Houses, it was burnt by the Common Hangman.

                                      Die

Die Lunæ 20. Maii 1661.

THE Lords in Parliament assembled, having considered of a Paper sent unto them from the House of Commons, for burning of the Instrument, or Writing, called The Solemn League, or Covenant, by the hands of the Common Hangman; Do Order, that the said Instrument, or Writing, called The Solemn League, and Covenant, be burned by the hand of the Common Hangman in the New-Palace at Westminster, in Cheapside, and before the Old Exchange on Wednesday the Twenty second of this instant May. And that the said Covenant be forthwith taken off the Record in the House of Peers, and in all other Courts, and Places, where the same is recorded; And that all Copies thereof be taken down out of all Churches, Chapels, and other publick places in England, and Wales, and in the Town of Barwick upon Twede, where the same are set up.

JO. BROWN

Cleric. Parliamentorum.

" *The Fourth hath on her Escutcheon an Arm, as it were out of the*
" *Clouds; in the Hand a naked Sword : the Motto,*

DISCITE JUSTITIAM MONITI.

Eight Mutes above, on Pedestals; four in White, four in Crimson.

The Musick of this Fabrick is ten Drummers, flanking REBELLION; twelve Trumpets flanking MONARCHY.

Aloft under the two Devastations, twelve Trumpets, four Drums.

Within the Arch, on two Balconies, six Trumpets, four Drums.

While the Train passeth along, the Drums beat the Marches of several Countries, and the Trumpets sound several *Levets.* At which Time His Majesty drawing near, the Drums turn their March to a Battel, the Trumpets sound a Charge, and on a sudden REBELLION rowseth up her Self, at which, Drums, and Trumpets ceasing, REBELLION addresses to His Majesty the following Speech.

Stand !

Stand! Stand! who 'ere You are! this Stage is Ours;
The Names of Princes are inscrib'd on Flow'rs,
And wither with them! Stand! You must Me know,
To Kings, and Monarchy a deadly Fo;
Me, who dare bid You 'midst Your Triumphs stand,
In the great City of Your Native Land :
I am Hell's Daughter, Satan's Eldest Child,
When I first cry'd, the Powers of Darkness smil'd,
And my Glad Father, Thund'ring at my Birth,
Unhing'd the Poles, and shook the fixed Earth.
My dear Rebellion (that shall be thy Name,
Said He) Thou Emperours, and Kings shalt tame,
No Right so good, Succession none so long,
But thou shalt vanquish by thy Popular Throng,
Those Legions, which t'enlarge our Pow'r we send
Throughout the World, shall Thee (my Dear) attend.
Our mighty Champions, the Sev'n Deadly Sins,
By Malice, Profit, Pleasure, all their Gins,
Bring to our Kingdom some few spotted Souls ;
Thou shalt by Treason burry them in Shoals.

  Would You now know what Int'rest I have here ?
Hydra I ride : great Cities are my Sphear :
I Sorc'ry use, and hang Men in their Beds,
With Common-wealths, and Rotas fill their Heads,
Making the Vulgar in Fanatique Swarms
Court Civil War, and dote on Horrid Arms ;
'Twas I, who, in the late unnatural Broils,
Engag'd three Kingdoms, and two Wealthy Isles :
I hope, at last, to march with Flags unfurl'd,
And tread down Monarchy through all the World.

            H   At

At which Words, *Monarchy*, and *Loyalty*, unveiling themselves, *Rebellion* starts as affrighted , but, recollecting her self, concludes her Speech thus.

> *Ah! Britain, Ah! stand'st thou Triumphant there,*
> *Monarchick Isle? I shake with horrid Fear.*
> *Are thy Wounds whole? Upon thy Cheek fresh Smiles?*
> *Is Joy restor'd to these late mournful Isles?*
> *Ah! must He enter, and a King be Crown'd?*
> *Then, as He riseth, sink we under Ground.*

Rebellion having ended her Speech , *Monarchy* entertains His Majesty with the following.

> *To Hell, foul Fiend, shrink from this glorious Light,*
> *And hide thy Head in everlasting Night.*
> *Enter in Safety, Royal Sir, this Arch,*
> *And through your joyful Streets in Triumph march ;*
> *Enter our Sun, our Comfort, and our Life.*
> *No more these Walls shall breed Intestine Strife :*
> *Henceforth Your People onely shall contend*
> *In Loyalty each other to transcend.*
> *May Your Great Actions, and immortal Name,*
> *Be the whole Business, and Delight of Fame.*
> *May You, and Yours, in a Perpetual Calm*
> *Be Crown'd with Laurel, and Triumphant Palm,*
> *And all Confess, whilst they in You are Blest,*
> *I, MONARCHY, of Governments am Best.*

Monarchy having ended her Speech , the Trumpets sound pleasant *Levets*, and the Drums beat a lofty *English* March, whilst His Majesty, the Nobility, and the Rear-Guard pass on.

The next Entertainment is at *Corn-hill*-Conduit , on the top of which stand eight *Nymphs* clad in White, each having an Escutcheon in one Hand, and a Pendent, or Banner in the other. On the Tower of the said Conduit, a Noise of seven Trumpets.

THE

Back of
Foldout
Not Imaged

THE SECOND ARCH.

NEAR the *Exchange*, in *Corn-hill*, is erected the Second *Arch*, which is *Naval*.

"On the East-*side* were *two Stages erected*; *on each side of the* "Street, *one*. In that on the South-*side was a Person representing the* "*River* Thames; *his Garment Loose, and Flowing, Colour Blew and* "*White, waved like Water*, a *Mantle over, like a Sail*; *his Head* "*crown'd with* London *Bridg, Flags, and Ozier, like long Hair, falling* "*o'ver his Shoulders, his Beard long, Sea-green, and White, curl'd*; *an* "*Oar in his right Hand, the Model of a Ship in his left, an Urn beside* "*him, out of which issued Water*; *four Attendants in White, represent-* "*ing the four fresh Streams, which fall into the River* Thames, *viz.* "Charwel, Lea, Coln, *and* Medway.

The Antients did very much differ in the Description of their Rivers, as *Ælian* * relates. *Those, that worship Rivers, and those, that make their Images, some form them in the likeness of Men, others in the likeness of* Oxen. *The* Stymphalians *liken the Rivers* Erasinus *and* Metope , *the* Lacedæmonians Eurotas , *the* Sicyonians *and* Phliasians Asopus, *the* Argives Cephissus, *unto* Oxen. *The* Psophidians *liken* Eryman-thus, *the* Herææans Alphæus, *the* Cherronesians, *that came from* Cni-dus, *the River* Cnidus, *to* Men. *The* Athenians *worship the River* Ce-phissus *under the form of a* Man, *but wearing Horns. In* Sicily *the* Syra-cusians *liken* Anapus *to a* Man, *but the Fountain* Cyane *to a* Woman. Virgil * *describes* Eridanus *in the Form of an Ox.*

* *Var. Hist. lib. ii. cap. xxxii.*

* *Georg. iv.*

> *Et gemina auratus taurino cornua vultu*
> *Eridanus, quo non alius per pinguia culta*
> *In mare purpureum violentior influit amnis.*

Golden

Golden *Eridanus*, with a double Horn,
Fac'd like a Bull, through fertile Fields of Corn,
Then whom, none swifter, of the *Ocean's* Sons,
Down to the Purple *Adriatick* runs.

On which place says *Probus*; *It's feign'd like a Bull, either because its noise is like the lowing of a Bull, or because its Banks are crooked like Horns.* The same says *Cornutus.* The *Scholiast* on *Sophocles* renders other reasons, either *because they cut the ground like Oxen ; or because Meadows, Pasture of Oxen, are always adjacent to them.* Horace; *tauriformis Aufidus.* So we finde in *Pindar* that the Bull, which *Perillus* gave to the Tyrant *Phalaris,* was the Image of the River *Gelon.* Very frequently we finde *Horns* attributed to them : as in *Virgil*,

> *Corniger* Hesperidum *fluvius regnator aquarum,*
> *Adsis ô tandem, propiùs tua numina firmes.*

Horn'd Flood, of all th' *Hesperian* Rivers King,
Now shew thy power, and us assistance bring.

Ovid,

> *Cornibus hic fractis, viridi malè tectus ab ulva,*
> *Decolor ipse suo, sanguine* Rhenus *erat.*

Here *Rhine* with Vine and Reeds ill cover'd stood,
His Horns being broke, distain'd with Native Blood.

Claudian,

> ———— Rhenúmque *minacem*
> *Cornibus infractis adeò mitescere cogis.*

> ———— and threatning *Ryne,*
His Horns being broke, thou did'st to Peace incline.

And again of *Eridanus,*

> ———— *ille caput placidis sublime fluentis*
> *Extulit, & totis lucem spargentia ripis.*

                                                                    Aurea

I Pyth.

Æn. lib. vi.

De laud. Stilicon. lib.

De vi. Consul. Honorii.

Aurea roranti micuerunt cornua vultu :
Non illi madidum vulgaris arundine crinem
Velat honos : rami caput umbravère virentes
Heliadum, totisque fluunt electra capillis.
Palla tegit latos humeros ; currùque paterno
Intextus Phaëthon glaucos incendit amictus.

Raiſing his Head above his Wat'ry Ranks,
His Golden Horns, reflecting, tip'd the Banks
With ſprinkled light. Drops trickling from his Face :
He his moiſt Hair veil'd not with Oziers baſe,
And vulgar Reeds : freſh Pop'lars Shade his Brows,
And Amber from his curled Treſſes flows.
A Robe his Shoulders hides ; *Phaethon's* wrought there :
His blew Veſt burning in his Father's Chair.

So we finde them also in the form of a *Man*   As the River *Rhene,*
as it is ſuppoſed : which Statue is ſtill extant in *Rome* lying in a Rock,
vulgarly call'd *Marforium* from *Mars's* Temple in *foro Auguſti*, his Hair
and Beard long, as if dropping with Water ; juſt as *Claudian* deſcribes   ↑ *De Prob.*
the River *Tyber,*   *& Olyb.*

Illi glauca nitent hirſuto lumina vultu, &c.
Diſtillant per pectus aquæ, frons hiſpida manat
Imbribus, in liquidos fontes ſe barva reſolvit.

His blew Eyes ſhine under his beetle Brows, &c.
His Fore-head ſwims, Water his Breaſt diſtills.
And his rough Beard diſſolves in Cryſtal Rills.

And

And the River *Danubius* in the Coyns of the Emperours *Trajan,* and *Conſtantine,*

Ceſar. p. 8.
Conſt. Tab.
XXX.

Their Heads were ordinarily environ'd with Reeds, Oziers, and the
like. *Ovid,* * relating the Fable of *Acis* turn'd into a River,

Metam. lib.
XIII.

> —————— *ſubitò medià tenùs extitit alvo*
> *Incinctus juvenu flexis nova cornua cannis.*

> From whence a Youth aroſe above the waſte,
> His horned Brows with quiv'ring Reeds imbrac't.

Æn. lib.
VIII.

Virgil, † of *Tyber,* the King of Rivers,

> *Huic Deus ipſe loci fluvio Tyberinus amœno*
> *Populeas inter ſenior ſe attollere frondes*
> *Viſus. Eum tenuis glauco velabat amictu*
> *Carbaſus, & crines umbroſa tegebat arundo.*

> The Genius of the Place, old *Tyber,* here
> Amongſt the Pop'lar Branches did appear.
> Of fineſt Linen were his Azure Weeds,
> And his moiſt Treſſes crown'd with ſhady Reeds.

where we may obſerve, that *Virgil* gives him a Sail for his Mantle.

De Prob. &
Olyb.

Claudian * of *Tyber,*
> —————— *criſpo denſantur gramine colla :*
> *Vertice luxuriat toto crinalis arundo,* &c.

> ——— *taurina*

—O—— taurina levantur
Cornua temporibus raucos sudantia rivos, &c.
Palla graves humeros velat, quam neverat uxor
Ilia, percurrens vitreas sub gurgite telas.

——— his Neck ripe Harvest bound ;
An interwoven Reed his Temples crown'd, &c.
——— And from his rising Horns distils
A Sweat, which swells to Crystal Rills, &c.
A Vest he wore, which *Ilia*, his Spouse
With Crystal Looms wove in her Wat'ry House.

OVID,

Metam.

——— capitis quoque fronde saligna
Aut superimposita celatur arundine damnum.

——— the damage of his Brows
He shades with flaggie Wreaths, and sallow Boughs.

The *Statue* indeed of the River *Tyber*, now extant in *Rome*, ha's its Head inviron'd with several sorts of Leaves, and Fruits, to signifie the fertility of the places near it, caused by the same : yet it recedes not so far from the Fiction of the *Poets*, but that it holds a Reed in its Hand. And the reason is, because these thrive best in watry places.

They are ordinarily described too leaning on an *Urn*, out of which issues Water.

VIRGIL, describing the Shield of *Turnus*,

Cælataque amnem fundens pater Inachus Urnâ.

And *Inachus* powrs Water from his *Urn*.

CLAUDIAN [†] of *Eridanus*,

† De vi. Cons ful. Honorii,

Fultáque sub gremio cælatis nobilis astris
Æthereum probat urna decus. ———

An

An Urn he bore, grav'd with Cœlestial Signs
That prov'd his high descent. ———

So is *Danubius* reprefented in the Coyns now mentioned. There is
a little Image of *Nile* leaning on its right Hand, with its left Hand
powring out Water from three Urns with one handle, about which
play fixteen little Children. Why *Nile* fhould be figured with three
Urns, this reafon is given: becaufe the *Ægyptian* Priefts attributed the
encreafe of it to three feveral caufes efpecially, rejecting all other opi-
nions, which were innumerable. The fixteen Children are the
Hieroglyphick of fixteen Cubits, the proper encreafe of the River
Nile : for, if it fwelled higher, it caufed dearth: for, by how much the
more it fwell'd, fo much the longer it was before it return'd into its
Channel, by which means the Seed-time was loft: if much under fifteen,
it irrigated not the whole Land, and fo part was unfit to receive Seed.
PLINY; *Juftum incrementum eft cubitorum fedecim. Minores aquæ non
omnia rigant; ampliores detinent, tardiùs recedendo. Hæ ferendi tempora
abfumunt, illæ non dant fitiente. Utrumque reputat Provincia. In duode-
cim cubitis famem fentit, in tredecim etiamnum efurit, quatuordecim cubita
hilaritatem afferunt, quindecim fecuritatem, fexdecim delicias.* There was
alfo not long fince a Marble *Colofs* of the River *Nile* digg'd up at
Rome with fixteen Infants playing about it. And fo doth *Philoftratus*
defcribe it.

Of the falling of the *Mole,* and *Medway* into the *Thames, Draigh-
ton* ha's feigned a pleafant Relation.

> *At length it came to pafs, that Ifis, and her* Tame,
> *Of* Medway *underftood, a* Nymph *of wond'rous Fame.*
> *And much defirous were their Princely* Tames *fhould prove*
> *If, as a Wooer, he could win her Maiden-love.*
> *That of fo great defcent, and of fo large a Dowver*
> *Might vvell allie their Houfe, and much encreafe his Power:*
> *And ftriving to prefer their Son the beft they may,*
> *Set forth the lufty Flood in rich and brave Array;*
> *Bank'd vvith imbroidered Meads, of fundry fuits of Flowrs,*
> *His Breaft adorn'd vvith Swans, oft vvafh'd vvith Silver Showrs:*

A

A Train of gallant Floods, at such a costly rate,
As might beseem their care, and fitting his Estate.

 Attended, and attired magnificently, thus
They send him to the Court of great Oceanus,
The World's huge Wealth to see ; yet with a full intent,
To woo the lovely Nymph, *fair* Medway, *as he went.*
Who to his Dame and Sire his duty scarce had done,
And whilst they sadly wept at parting of their Son,
See what the Tames *befel, when 'twas suspected least.*

 As still his goodly Train yet ev'ry hour encreast,
And from the Surrian *Shores clear* Wey *came down to meet*
His Greatness, whom the Tames *so graciously doth greet,*
That with the Fearn-crown'd Flood he, Minion*-like, doth play ;*
Yet is not this the Brook enticeth him to stay :
But, as they thus in pomp came sporting on the shole,
'Gainst Hampton-Court *he meets the soft and gentle* Mole;
Whose eyes so pierc'd his Breast, that seeming to foreslow
The way, which he so long intended was to go,
With trifling up and down he wandreth here and there,
And that he in her sight transparent might appear,
Applies himself to Fords, and setteth his delight
On that, which most might make him gracious in her sight.

 Then Isis *and the* Tame *from their conjoyned Bed,*
Desirous still to learn how Tames *their Son had sped,*
(For greatly they had hop'd, his time had so been spent,
That he e're this had won the goodly Heir of Kent)
And, sending to enquire, had News return'd again
(By such as they employ'd on purpose in his Train)
How this their onely Heir, the Isle's *imperial Flood,*
Had loiter'd thus in love, neglectful of his good.

 No mervail at the News, though Owse *and* Tame *were sad,*
More comfort of their Son expecting to have had.
       I

             Nor

Nor blame them, in their looks much sorrow though they show'd,
Who, fearing lest he might thus meanly be bestow'd,
And knowing danger still increased by delay,
Employ their utmost pow'r to hasten him away.
But Tames would hardly on : oft turning back to show,
From his much-lov'd Mole how loth he was to go.
The Mother of the Mole, old Homes-dale, likewise bears
The affection of her Childe, as ill as they do theirs :
Who, nobly though deriv'd, yet could have been content,
T'have match'd her with a Flood of far more mean descent.
But Mole respects her words, as vain and idle Dreams,
Compar'd with that high joy to be belov'd of Tames ;
And head-long holds her course his Company to win :
But Homes-dale raised Hills, to keep the stragler in ;
That of her Daughter's stay she need no more to doubt :
(Yet never was there help, but Love could finde it out.)
Mole digs her self a Path, by working Day and Night,
(According to her Name, to shew her Nature right)
And underneath the Earth for three miles space doth creep,
Till gotten out of sight, quite from her Mother's keep,
Her fore-intended course the wanton Nymph doth run,
As longing to embrace old Tame and Isis Son.

When Tames now understood, what pains the Mole did take,
How far the loving Nymph adventur'd for his sake ;
Although with Medway match'd, yet never could remove
The often-quickning sparks of his more antient love.
So that it comes to pass, when by great Nature's guide
The Ocean doth return, and thrusteth-in the Tide,
Up, tow'rds the place, where first his much-lov'd Mole was seen,
He ever since doth flow, beyond delightful Sheen.

Mr. DRAYTON in his *Poly-Olbion.*

"In

" *In the other Stage on the North-side, which is made like the upper Deck*
" *of a Ship, were three Sea-men, whereof one habited like a Boat-*
" *Swain.*

" *A Shield, or Table, in the Front of the Arch, bears this* Inscription,

NEPTUNO BRITANNICO,

CAROLO II,

CUJUS ARBITRIO

MARE

VEL LIBERUM, VEL CLAUSUM·

The Dominion of the Sea (signified here by this *Inscription*) ha's been
in all Ages so remarkable, that, when the *Grecian Chronographers* could
finde no Foot-step of Supreme Empire by Land, before the institution
of their *Olympiads*, on whose Actions they could found their *Chronogra-*
phy, they directed the Series of Time according to the succession of
those Nations, who had the Empire of the Sea : which we see in † *Eu-*
sebius ; who reckons up nine several Nations, who successively held it,
before the institution of the *Olympiads*, and distinctly enumerates the
years they retain'd it. The same right the *Grecians* challenged in their
League with *Artaxerxes*, King of a vast part of A s i a, after the over-
throw of his Naval Forces by *Cimon* the *Athenian Admiral*, ἵππῳ μὴ ἐφ᾽ οἷς
ἐπὶ ὁ Ἑλληνικὸς ἀπέχει θαλάσσης, ἤλον μὴ πλεῖον ἢ Χελιδωνίων μαχρὶ τὴ μὴ πλεῖν. *That*
he should not within a Horse Race approach the Greek *Sea, nor sail within*
the Cyanean, *and* Chelidonian *Islands with any Man of War*. The same
Dominion of the Sea was afterwards assumed by the *Romans*, as we finde
by the Commission granted to *Pompey*, Ἄρχειν ᾗ ὁ τῆς Ἡρακλείων στηλῶν θαλάσσης
ἁπάσης ἡ πάσης ἐπὶ γαλήνης πιτραχεθὼς τῆν ἔκλάσσνος· *That he should have the Em-*
pire of the Sea within the Streights, and of the Continent for four hundred
Stadia from the Sea. And not long after *Dionysius Halicarnassæus* says, *
That *Rome* was *Empress of the whole Sea, not onely of that within the*
Streights,

I 2

† *Christ.*

* *Orig. Rom.*
Lib. 3.

Streights, *but of the Ocean it self, as far as it was Navigable.* Whence *Augustus* had a *Dolphin* in his Coyns to signifie that Dominion,

And * *Valerius Maximus* to *Tiberius* the Emperour, *The Consent both of Gods and Men ha's constituted you Governour of Sea, and Land.* Afterwards *Claudian* [1],

> ―――― *terræ dominos pelagique futuros,*
> *Immenso decuit rerum de Principe nasci.*

> Those, who must rule both Sea, and Land,
> Ought to be Princes Sons of great Command.

And sure, if any Nation may plead Prescription for this Title, the *King* of ENGLAND may, having had a longer uninterrupted Succession in the Dominion of the BRITTISH *Seas,* then the ROMANS in the *Mediterranean,* or any other Nation, that *History* ha's acquainted us with. The Antiquity whereof being purposely, and at large declared by Mr. SELDEN, we shall onely take notice of two *Records* of it, the one taken out of the *Laws* of *Hoëlus Dha,* Prince of WALES, about the Year, 982. viz. *Quos cum Cunadio Rege Scotorum, Malcolmo Rege Cambrorum, & Maccusio Archipirata, ad civitatem Legionum sibi occurrentes, Rex Anglorum Eadgarus in Triumphi pompam deducebat. Una enim impositos remigrare eos hanc coegit, dum in Prora ipse sedens Navis tennit gubernaculum : ut se hoc spectaculo Soli & Sali orbis Britannici Dominum prædicaret, & Monarcham.* The other is a Record in the Tower of *London,* entituled *De superioritate maris Angliæ,* &c. in which it evidently appears, that the Dominion of the *Brittish* Seas belong'd to the Kings of *England* time out of mind, even before *Edward* the First, and was so acknowledged by other Neighbouring Nations; out of which

In Prolegg.
De vi Consul. Honori.

which we shall onely extract so much as may serve for our present purpose, viz. *That the Procuratours of the Admiral of the Sea of England, and of other places, as of the Sea Coasts, as of Genoa, Catalonia, Spain, Almain, Zealand, Holland, Freezland, Denmark, and Norway, do shew that the Kings of England, time out of mind, have been in peaceable possession of the Seas of England, in making and establishing Laws, and Statutes, and Restraints of Arms, and of Ships, &c and in taking Surety, &c. and in ordering all other things necessary for the maintaining of Peace, Right, and Equity, &c. and in doing Justice, Right, and Law, according to the said Laws, Ordinances, and Restraints, and in all other things, which may appertain to the exercise of Sovereign Dominion in the places aforesaid.*

" *The first Painting on the North side over the City-Arms, represents* " NEPTUNE, *with his Trident advanced; the Inscription,*

NEPTUNO REDUCI.

NEPTUNE's Statue is seldom seen without a Trident in its hand. *Pausanias* [†], *Within the Temple there is an erect Brazen Statue (of* NEPTUNE) *with one foot upon a* Dolphin, *and on that side his Hand on his Thigh ; in his other Hand a* Trident. And so he is every where described by the Poets.   † In Phocicis.

Perque tuum, pater Ægei Neptune, *Tridentem.*

But more of this hereafter.

The Motto NEPTUNO REDUCI we finde in two Medaigles, the one of the Emperour *Adrian,* the other of *Vespasian,* with these Letters on one side NEPT. RED. and the image of one standing naked, a Mantle on his left Shoulder, in his right Hand a Whip with three Cords, in his left a Trident.

" *On the South-side, opposite,* MARS, *with his Spear inverted, his Shield* " *charged with a Gorgon ; by his Knees, the Motto,*

MARTI PACIFERO.

So

So HOMER deſcribes the Shield of *Agamemnon*,

Τῇ δ' ἐπὶ μὲν Γοργὼ βλοσυρῶπις ἐςεφάνωτο,
Δωὸν δερκομένη, περὶ δὲ Δειμός τε φόβΘ τε.

The Sable Field charg'd with a Gorgon's *Head,*
Mantled about with diſmal Flight, and Dread:

and in another place the Armour of *Pallas,*

Ἐν δέ τε Γοργείη Κεφαλὴ δεινοῖο πελώρου,
Δεινή τε σμερδνή τε, Διὸς τέρας αἰγιόχοιο.

Amidſt, that horrid Monſter Gorgon's *Head,*
Jove's direſt Omen, fierce, and full of dread.

Pauſanias ; *Under the Statue of Victory lies a* Golden Shield, *with a*
Gorgon *wrought upon it.* And it is obſerv'd by the *Scholiaſt* on * *Ari-*
ſtophanes, that it was Cuſtomary among the *Grecians* to have a *Gorgon's*
Head on their Shields, as he repreſents ¹ *Lamachus's.* The Form of
this *Gorgon's* Head is ſtill to be ſeen at *Rome* on the Statues of the Emperours *Veſpaſian* and *Domitian.* It was feigned with Wings, to ſignifie the preſent death, that attended it : for whoever looked on it, immediatly was turn'd into Stone. The which at large , and very elegantly is declared by *Ovid,*

> *But when he ſaw his Valour overſway'd*
> *By* Multitude ; *I muſt, ſaid he, ſeek aid*
> *(Since you your ſelves compell me) from my Foe ;*
> *Friends turn your Back: then* Gorgon's *Head doth ſhow.*
> *Some others ſeek, ſaid* Theſſalus, *to fright*
> *With this thy Monſter, and with all his might*
> *A deadly Dart endeavour'd to have thrown :*
> *But in that Poſiture became a Stone.*
> Next Amphix, *full of ſpirit, forward preſt,*
> *And thruſt his Sword at bold* Lyncides Breaſt :

When

In Achaia.
¹ *In Pace.*

Metam.
lib. v. Fab. i.

When in the Pass his Fingers stupid grow,
Nor had the pow'r of moving to or fro.
But Nileus (he, who with a forged stile
Vaunted to be the Son of sev'n-fold Nile,
And bare sev'n Silver Rivers in his Shield,
Distinctly waving through a Golden Field)
To Perseus said; Behold, from whence we sprung !
To ever-silent Shadows bear along
This comfort of thy Death, that thou did'st die
By such a brave, and high-born Enemy.
His utt'rance faulter'd in the latter Clause,
The yet unfinish'd Word stuck in his Jaws;
Who gaping stood, as he would something say,
And so had done, if words had found a way.
These Eryx blames; 'Tis your faint Souls, that dead
Your Pow'rs, said he, and not the Gorgon's Head:
Rush on with me, and prostrate with deep Wounds
This Youth, who thus with Magick Arms confounds.
Then rushing on, the ground his foot-steps stai'd
Now mutely fix'd, an armed Statue made.

    These suffer'd worthily. One, who did fight
For Perseus, bold Aconteus, at the sight
Of Gorgon's Snakes abortive Marble grew,
On whom Astyages in fury flew,
As if alive, with his two-handled Blade,
Which shrilly twang'd, but no incision made.
Who, whilst he wonders, the same Nature took,
And now his Statue ha's a wondring look.
It were too tedious for me to report
Their Names, who perish'd of the vulgar sort:

                                    Two

Two hundred scap'd the fury of the Fight;
Two hundred turn'd to stone at Gorgon's *sight.*

Mr. SANDYS.

⸸ Epithal.
Pal.

The Head is thus described ⸸ by SIDONIUS APOLLINARIS,

Gorgo *tenet pectus medium, factura videnti*
Et truncata moras, nitet insidiosa superbum
Effigies, vivitque animâ pereunte venustas.
Alta cerastarum spiris caput asperat atrum
Congeries, torquet maculosa volumina mordax
Crinis, & irati dant sibila tetra capilli.

The *Gorgon's* Head, which guards her Bosome, would
Change thee to Statue, should'st thou it behold.
The treach'rous Face shows proudly, and, though dead,
Life's beauty keeps. Snakes, matted round her Head,
In speckled Curls voluminously wreath,
And biting Tresses direly-hissing breath.

⸸ In Arcad.

PAUSANIAS * reports, that *Pallas* made a City impregnable,
by communicating onely a little Hair cut off from her *Gorgon's* Head.

The Title of PACIFER is attributed to *Mars* in the *Roman*
Coyns; as in this of *Quintillus,*

Holstat.

So we finde, that the *Romans* erected a Temple to *Mars Quirinus,* as
well as *Mars Gradivus.* The first had his Temple within the City:
the

the other without in the *Appian*-way, not far from the Gate. The one, with a gentle, sedate Countenance, to preserve the tranquillity, and peace of the City: the other, to go out with them in their Wars abroad. *Gellius* * says, *That* Hersila *speaking before* T. Tatius, *and desiring Peace, prayed on this manner,* O Neria, *Wife of* Mars, *I beseech thee to grant us Peace, that we may enjoy a during, and prosperous Marriage.* And therefore the Olive, the Symbole of Peace, was consecrated to *Pallas,* the Goddess of War; because War is therefore undertaken, that a secure Peace may be enjoyed. *Ideò arma inferri dicuntur, ut posteà in pace vivatur,* says *Pliny.*

* *Noct. Att. Lib.* xiii.

" *Over the Arch, the Marriage of* Thame *and* Isis.

The Marriage of Rivers is a frequent Fiction among the Poets: as of *Alpheus* and *Arethusa*; therefore feign'd, because *Alpheus,* a River of *Elis* in the *Morea*, passeth through the *Ocean*, unmix'd, to the River *Arethusa* in the Island *Ortygia*, near *Syracuse*, a City of *Sicily*. Which passage ha's been often tried, as by a Cup, says † *Strabo*, let fall in the River *Alpheus* in *Elis*, and found in *Arethusa*: maintain'd also by an *Oracle* given to *Archias,* a *Corinthian,* that he should thither deduce a *Colony,* where *Alpheus* is mingled with the Fountain of *Arethusa*. The Marriage of these two we have described by * O v i d, where the Nymph *Arethusa* speaks, being ready to be turn'd into a River;

† *Geog. Lib.* vi.

* *Metam. Lib.* v.

> *Cold Sweats my then-besieged Limbs possess't:*
> *In thin thick-falling Drops my strength decreas't.*
> *Where e're I step, Streams run; my Hair now fell*
> *In trickling Dew; and, sooner then I tell*
> *My Destiny, into a Flood I grew.*
> *The River his beloved Waters knew;*
> *And, putting off th'assumed shape of Man,*
> *Resumes his own, and in my Current ran.*
> *Chast Delia cleft the ground: then, through blind Caves,*
> *To lov'd Ortygia she conducts my Waves,*
> *Affected for her Name: where first I take*
> *Review of day. This Arethusa spake.*

                                      Mr. SANDYS.
              K.   Thus

Ibid. Thus *Anapus*, and *Cyane* are feign'd mutual Lovers ; because their Waters unite, and run together into the Sea. Ovid,

> ———— *quòd si componere magnis*
> *Parva mihi fas est ; & me dilexit* Anapus :
> *Exorata tamen, nec, ùt hæc, exterrita nupsi.*

> If humble things I may compare with great,
> *Anapus* lov'd me ; yet did he intreat,
> And me, not frighted thus, espous'd.

The Marriage of *Tibur* and *Ilia* is frequently mention'd,   Ovid, speaking of both,

> *Atque ità se in rapidas perdita misit aquas :*
> *Supposuisse manus ad pectora lubricus amnis*
> *Dicitur, & socii jura dedisse thori.*

> She leap'd amidst the Stream with grief opprest :
> The River puts his hand beneath her Breast,
> And, as they say, unloos'd her Virgin-Cest.

In another place,
> *Nec te prætereo, qui, per cava saxa volutus,*
> Tiburis Argæi *spumifer arva rigas :*
> Ilia *cui placuit.*————

> Nor thee, roll'd through worn Rocks, do I pass by,
> Who on *Tyburtian* Grounds dost foaming ly :
> Whom *Ilia* pleas'd. ————

Lib. xii. SILIUS ITALICUS,
> *Ad genitorem* Anio *labens sine murmure* Tibrim.
> *Hic, ùt signa ferox, dimensáque castra locavit,*

Et

Et ripas tremefecit eques, perterrita pulfis
Ilia prima vadis facro fe conjugis antro
Condidit.————

———— but on, like a rude Storm, he goes
To thofe low Banks, where *Anio* gently flows
With Sulph'rous Waters, and with Silence, to
Old *Tiber's* Arms; when here the Line he drew
Of's Camp, and fet his Standard up, and fhook
His Banks with's Cavalry, firft *Ilia*, ftrook
With Fear, flies to her Husband's facred Cave,
And all the frighted *Nymphs* the Water leave.

                    Mr. R o s s.

The Marriage of *Tame* and *Ifis*, here mention'd, is pleafantly related by Mr. D r a y t o n ;

In his Po-
ly-Olbion,
Sing 15.

Now Fame had through this Ile divulg'd, in every ear,
The long-expected day of Marriage to be near,
That *Ifis*, *Cotfwold's* Heir, long-woo'd, was laftly won,
And inftantly fhould wed with *Tame*, old *Chiltern's* Son.
   And now that Wood-man's Wife, the Mother of the Flood,
The rich and goodly Vale of *Alefbury*, that ftood
So much upon her *Tame*, was bufied in her Bow'rs,
Preparing for her Son as many Sutes of Flow'rs,
At *Cotfwold* for the Bride, his *Ifis*, lately made;
Who for the lovely *Tame*, her Bridegroom, onely ftaid.
   Whilft every Cryftal Flood is to this bufinefs preft,
The caufe of their great fpeed and many thus requeft;
O! whither go ye Floods? what fuddain Winde doth blow,
Then other of your kind that you fo faft fhould flow?

              K 2   What

What bufinefs is in hand, that fpurs you thus away?
Fair *Windrufh*, let me hear, I pray thee, *Charwel* fay:
They fuddainly reply, What lets, you fhould not fee,
That for this Nuptial Feaft we all prepared be?
Therefore this idle chat our Ears doth but offend;
Our leifure ferves not now thefe Trifles to attend.
   But, whilft things are in hand, old *Chiltern* (for his life)
From prodigal expenfe can no way keep his Wife;
Who feeds her *Tame* with Marl, in Cordial-wife prepar'd,
And thinks all idly fpent, that now fhe onely fpar'd
In fetting forth her Son: nor can fhe think it well,
Unlefs her lavifh charge do *Cotfwold*'s far exeel.
For *Alesbury*'s a Vale, that walloweth in her Wealth,
And (by her wholefom Air continually in health)
Is lufty, trim, and fat, and holds her youthful ftrength.
Befides her fruitful Earth, her mighty breadth, and length,
Doth *Chiltern* fitly match: which mountainoufly high,
And being very long, fo likewife fhe doth lie;
From the *Bedfordian* Fields, where firft fhe doth begin,
To fafhion like a Vale, to th'place where *Tame* doth win
His *Ifis* wifhed Bed; her Soil throughout fo fure,
For goodnefs of her Glebe, and for her Pafture pure,
That as her Grain, and Grafs, fo fhe her Sheep doth breed,
For Burthen, and for Bone, all other that exceed:
And fhe, which thus in Wealth abundantly doth flow,
Now cares not on her Childe what coft fhe do beftow.
Which when wife *Chiltern* faw (the World who long had try'd,
And now at laft had laid all garifh Pomp afide;
Whofe hoar and chalky Head defcri'd him to be old,
His Beechen Woods bereft, that kept him from the Cold)
Would fain perfwade the Vale to hold a fteddy rate;
And with his curious Wife thus wifely doth debate:
                          Quoth

Quoth he, you might allow what needeth, to the most :
But where as less will serve, what means this idle Cost ?
Too much a Surfet breeds, and may our Childe annoy :
These fat and lushious Meats do but our Stomacks cloy.
The modest comely mean in all things likes the Wise,
Apparel often shews us Womanish precise.
And what will *Cotswold* think, when he shall hear of this ?
He'l rather blame your Waste, then praise your Cost, I wiss,

But, Women wilful be, and she her Will must have,
Nor cares how *Chiltern* chides, so that her *Tame* be brave.
Alone which tow'rds his Love she easily doth convay ;
For the *Oxonian Owse* was lately sent away
From *Buckingham*, where first he finds his nimbler Feet ;
Tow'rds *Whittlewood* then takes : where, past the noblest Street,
He to the Forest gives his farewel, and doth keep
His course directly down into the *German* Deep,
To publish that great day in mighty *Neptune*'s Hall,
That all the Sea-gods there might keep it Festival.

As we have told how *Tame* holds on his even course,
Return we to report, how *Isis* from her sourse
Comes tripping with delight, down from her daintier Springs ;
And in her Princely Train, t'attend her Marriage, brings
Clear *Churnet, Coln*, and *Leech*, which first she did retain,
With *Windrush* : and with her (all out-rage to restrain,
Which well might offered be to *Isis*, as she went)
Came *Yenload* with a Guard of *Satyres*, which were sent
From *Whichwood*, to await the bright and God-like Dame,
So *Bernwood* did bequeath his *Satyres* to the *Tame*,
For Sticklers in those stirs, that at the Feast should be.

These Preparations great when *Charwel* comes to see,
To *Oxford* got before, to entertain the Flood,
Apollo's Aid he begs, with all his sacred Brood,

To

To that most learned place to welcome her repair,
Who in her coming on was wax'd so wond'rous fair,
That, meeting, strife arose betwixt them, whether they
Her Beauty should extol, or she admire their Bay.
On whom their sev'ral gifts (to amplifie her Dower)
The *Muses* there bestow ; which ever have the power
Immortal her to make. And, as she past along,
Those modest *Thespian* Maids thus to their *Isis* song.

Ye Daughters of the Hills, come down from every side,
And due attendance give upon the lovely Bride :
Go strew the Paths with Flowers, by which she is to pass :
For be ye thus assur'd, in *Albion* never was
A Beauty (yet) like hers : where have ye ever seen
So absolute a *Nymph* in all things, for a Queen ?
Give instantly in charge the day be wond'rous fair,
That no disorder'd Blast attempt her braided Hair.
Go, see her State prepar'd, and every thing be fit,
The Bride-Chamber adorn'd with all beseeming it.
And for the Princely Groom, who ever yet could name
A Flood, that is so fit for *Isis*, as the *Tame* ?
Ye both so lovely are, that knowledge scarce can tell,
For Feature whether he, or Beauty she excel :
That, ravished with joy each other to behold,
When as your Crystal Wasts you closely do enfold,
Betwixt your beauteous selves you shall beget a Son,
That when your lives shall end, in him shall be begun.
The pleasant *Surrian* Shores shall in that Flood delight,
And *Kent* esteem her self most happy in his sight.
The Shire that *London* loves, shall onely him prefer,
And give full many a gift to hold him near to her.
The *Skeld*, the goodly *Mose*, the rich and Viny *Rhein*,
Shall come to meet the *Thames* in *Neptune*'s watry Plain.

                                                    And

And all the *Belgian* Streams, and neighb'ring Floods of *Gaul*,
Of him shall stand in aw, his Tributaries all.

As of fair *Isis* thus the learned Virgins spake,
A shrill and suddain Bruit this *Prothalamion* brake;
That *White-horse*, for the love she bare to her Ally,
And honoured Sister-Vale, the bounteous *Alesbury*,
Sent Presents to the *Tame*, by *Ock* her onely Flood,
Which for his Mother-Vale so much on greatness flood.

From *Oxford Isis* hasts more speedily, to see
That River, like his Birth, might entertained be :
For that ambitious Vale, still striving to command,
And using for her place continually to stand,
Proud *White-horse* to perswade much business there hath been,
T'acknowledge that great Vale of *Eusham* for her Queen.
And but that *Eusham* is so opulent, and great,
That thereby she her self holds in the Sovereign Seat,
This *White-horse* all the Vales of *Britain* would or'ebear,
And absolutely sit in the Imperial Chair ;
And boasts as goodly Heards, and num'rous Flocks to feed,
To have as soft a Glebe, as good increase of Seed ;
As pure and fresh an Ayr upon her Face to flow,
As *Eusham* for her life : and from her Steed doth show,
Her lusty rising Downs as fair a Prospect take,
As that imperious *Wold* ; which her great Queen doth make
So woud'rously admir'd, and her so far extend.
But to the Mariage, hence, industrious Muse descend.

The *Naiads*, and the *Nymphs* extremely over-joy'd,
And on the winding Banks all busily imploy'd,
Upon this joyful day, some dainty Chaplets twine ;
Some others chosen out, with fingers neat and fine,
Brave Anadems do make : some Bauldricks up do bind ;
Some, Garlands : and to some the Nosegays were assign'd ;

                                                    As

As best their Skill did serve. But, for that *Tame* should be
Still man-like as himself, therefore they will, that he
Should not be dreft with Flow'rs, to Gardens that belong,
(His Bride that better fit) but onely such as sprong
From the replenish'd Meads, and fruitful Paftures near:
To fort which Flow'rs fome fit; fome making Garlands were;
The Primrofe placing first, because that in the Spring
It is the first appears, then onely flourishing;
The azur'd Hare-bell next with them they neatly mixt:
T'allay whofe lushious Smell they Woodbind plac'd betwixt.
Amongst thofe things of fcent, there prick they in the Lilly;
And near to that again her Sifter Daffadilly.
To fort thefe Flow'rs of fhow with th'other that were fweet,
The Cowflip then they couch, and th'Oxflip,for her meet:
The Columbine amongst they fparingly do fet,
The Yellow King-cup, wrought in many a curious fret,
And now and then among, of Eglantine a fpray,
By which again a courfe of Lady-fmocks they lay:
The Crow-flower, and thereby the Clover-flower they ftick.
The Dayfie over all thofe fundry fweets fo thick,
As Nature doth her felf; to imitate her right:
Who feems in that her Pearl fo greatly to delight,
That ev'ry Plain therewith fhe powd'reth to behold:
The crimfon Darnel Flow'r, the Blew-bottle, and Gold;
Which though efteem'd but Weeds, yet for their dainty hews,
And for their fcent not ill, they for their purpofe chufe.

    Thus having told you how the Bridegroom *Tame* was dreft,
I'le fhew you how the Bride, fair *Ifis*, they inveft;
Sitting to be attir'd under her Bow'r of State,
Which fcorns a meaner fort, then fits a Princely rate.
In Anadems, for whom they curioufly difpofe
The Red, the dainty White, the goodly Damask Rofe,

                            For

For the rich Ruby, Pearl, and Amatiſt, men place
In Kings Emperial Crowns, the Circle that enchaſe.
The brave Carnation then, with ſweet and ſoveraign power
(So of his colour call'd, although a July-flower)
With th'other of his kind, the ſpeckled and the pale :
Then th'odoriferous Pink, that ſends forth ſuch a Gale
Of ſweetneſs ; yet in ſcents, as various as in ſorts.
The Purple Violet then, the Panſie there ſupports :
The Mary-gold above t'adorn the arched Bar ;
The double Dayſie, Thriſt, the Button-batcheler,
Sweet William, Sops in Wine, the Campion : and to theſe,
Some Lavander they put, with Roſemary and Bays :
Sweet Marjoram, with her like, ſweet Baſil rare for ſmell,
With many a Flower, whoſe name were now too long to tell :
And rarely with the reſt, the goodly Flower-delice.

Thus for the nuptial hour, all fitted point-device,
Whilſt ſome ſtill buſied are in decking of the Bride,
Some others were again as ſeriouſly imploy'd
In ſtrewing of thoſe Hearbs, at Bridals us'd that be :
Which every where they throw with bounteous hands and free.
The healthful Balm and Mint, from their full laps do fly,
The ſcent-ful Camomil, the verdurous Coſtmary.
They hot Muſcado oſt with milder Maudlin caſt :
Strong Tanſey, Fennel cool, they prodigally waſte :
Clear Iſop, and therewith the comfortable Thyme,
Germander with the reſt, each thing then in her prime ;
As well of wholeſome Hearbs, as every pleaſant Flower,
Which Nature here produc'd, to fit this happy hour.
Amongſt theſe ſtrewing kinds, ſome other wilde that grow,
As Burnet, all abroad, and Meadow-wort they throw.

L

"The

" *The Painting on the* North-*side* , *over* **Neptune**, *represents th*ᵉ
" **EXCHANGE**; *the Motto*,

——GENERIS LAPSI SARCIRE RUINAS.

" *An Expression of* Virgil's, *in the fourth of his* Georgicks, *speaking*
" *of the Industry of* Bees, *never discouraged by their Losses*; *his Descri-*
" *ption of it running thus,*

> *Quò magis exhaustæ fuerint, hoc acriùs omnes*
> *Incumbent generis lapsi sarcire ruinas,*
> *Complebuntque Foros, & Floribus Horrea texent.*

> How much by Fortune they exhausted are,
> So much they strive the Ruins to repair
> Of their fal'n Nation, and they fill th' *Exchange*,
> Adorning with the choicest Flow'rs their Grange.

" *The Painting on the* South-*side, over* Mars, *shews the* TOWER *of*
" London ; *the* Inscription,

CLAUDUNTUR BELLI PORTÆ.

This is in reference to the *Temple* of JANUS , never shut, but in the
time of *Peace* ; nor opened, but in time of *War*. Therefore, when
King *Latinus* had refused to raise a War against *Æneas*, and his
Followers, and to that purpose, to open the Gates of the *Temple* of
JANUS, *Juno*, resolving to have a War prosecuted against him,
opened them her self : mention'd by VIRGIL [†].

[†] *Æneid*.vii.

> *Hoc & tum* Æneadis *indicere bella* Latinus
> *More jubebatur, tristéíque* RECLUDERE PORTAS.
> *Abstinuit tactu Pater, aversisque refugit*
> *Fœda ministeria, & cæcis se condidit umbris.*
> *Tum Regina Deûm, cælo delapsa, morantes*
> *Impulit ipsa manu* PORTAS : *&, cardine verso,*
> *Belli ferratos rupit* Saturnia *postes.*

The

The King was here required by the States
War to denounce, and OPEN JANUS GATES.
He flies th' Engagement, and so foul a Cause,
And straight himself to privacy withdraws.
Then from high Heav'n the Queen of Gods descends,
And the resisting Portals open rends.
She breaks the Hinges, tears down Iron Bars,
And makes a spacious way for impious Wars.

" *The Pedestals, in the Upper Story, are adorned with eight living Fi-*
" *gures, representing* EUROPE, ASIA, AFRICK, *and* AMERICA, *with*
" *Escutcheons, and Pendents, bearing the Arms of the* Companies *trading*
" *into those parts.*

"EUROPE, *a Woman arm'd* a l'antique ; *on her Shield a Woman ri-*
" *ding on a Bull* ; *at her foot a* Coney.

The Effigies of *Europe* in Armour relates to the Warlike disposition
of that part of the World, evidently seen in the *Greek,* and *Roman* Mo-
narchies. We shall not need to describe her Armour in particular, but
leave it to be taken from this Description of *Rome,* the Mistress of *Eu-*
rope, in *Claudian,*

Ipsa, triumphatis quæ possidet æthera regnis,
Assilit, innuptæ ritus imitata Minervæ :
Nam neque cæsariem crinali stringere cultu
Colla, nec ornatu patitur mollire retorto ;
Dextrum nuda latus, niveos exserta lacertos,
Audacem retegit mammam, laxúmque coërcens
Mordet gemma sinum : nodus, qui sublevat ensem,
Album puniceo pectus discriminat ostro.
Miscetur decori virtus, pulchérque severo
Armatur terrore pudor, galeæque minaci
Flava cruentarum prætenditur umbra jubarum.
Et formidato clypeus Titana *lacessit*
Lumine, quem totá variárat Mulciber *arte.*

L 2   She

She who by conquering Realms the Sky poſſeſt,
Starts from her Seat, like Virgin-*Pallas* dreſt :
Her Hair no Fillet bound, nor was her Head
Dreſt up, Treſſes hung o're her Shoulders ſpread,
Her right ſide nak'd, with ſtretch'd out Arms, her Breaſt
Boldly ſhe bares, a Jemme claſpt up her Veſt,
Her Faulchion in a Purple Belt, more bright
Her Boſom rendred, ſetting off the white :
Valour with Beauty mix'd, a modeſt Bluſh
With terrour arm'd, her threatning Cask and Buſh
Of Bloody Plumage caſt a dreadful ſhade :
And *Gorgon*-Shield, that *Titan* ſo diſmai'd,
Which *Vulcan* with ſuch art and labour made.

Whom *Sidonius Apollinaris* followed ſo nearly, that there will need no
other Tranſlation then the precedent.

Sederat exerto bellatrix pectore Roma
Criſtatum turrita caput, cui ponè capaci
Caſſide prolapſus perfundit terga capillus.
Lætitia cenſura manet, terrorque pudore
Creſcit, & invitâ ſuperat virtute venuſtas.
Oſtricolor pepli textus, quem fibula torto
Mordax dente vorat, tum quicquid mamma refundit
Tegminis, hoc patulo concluſit gemma receſſu.
Hinc fulcit rutilus ſpacioſo circite lævum
Umbo latus, videas hic craſſo fuſa metallo
Antra Rheæ, fœtamq; lupam, quam ſauce retecta
Blandiri quoq; terror erat, quanquam illa vorare
Martigenas & picta timet, pars proxima Tybrin
Exprimit; hic ſcabri fuſus ſub pumice tophi
Proflabat madidum per guttura glauca ſoporem.

Panegyr. Majoriano.

Her

Her Shield comprehends the Story from whence *Europe* had her name, agreeably to the Custome of the Ancients : as we finde by this description of the Shield of *Rome* in the same Authour.   *Ibid.*

> *Hic patrius Mavortis amor, fœtusq; notantur*
> *Romulei ; post amnis inest, & bellua nutrix.*
> *Electro Tyberis, Pueri formantur in Auro.*
> *Tingunt æra lupam, Mavors adamante coruscat.*

> Here *Mars* escapes, and there the Twins he drew,
> And next the River, and the Shee-wolfe too:
> *Tyber* in Amber, and the Boyes in Gold,
> The Wolf in Brass, *Mars* he in Steel did mould.

The first part of which seems to be taken from that of *Æneas* in *Virgil*,

> *Illic res Italas, Romanórumque triumphos,*
> *Haud vatum ignarus venturique inscius ævi,*
> *Fecerat Ignipotens, illic genus omne futuræ*
> *Stirpis ab Ascanio, pugnataque in ordine bello*
> *Fecerat, & viridi fœtam Mavortis in antro*
> *Procubuisse lupam ; geminos huic ubera circum*
> *Ludere pendentes pueros, & lambere matrem*
> *Impavidos ; illam tereti cervice reflexam*
> *Mulcere alternos, & corpora fingere linguâ,*
> *Nec procul hinc, Romam, &c.*

> Th' Ignipotent God, well skill'd in Fates to come,
> The *Roman* triumphs and affaires of *Rome*,
> There had engrav'd, *Ascanius* Off-spring wrought,
> And all their bloody battels must be fought.
> The pregnant Wolfe in *Mars* green Covert lay,
> And hanging at her breasts two Infants play:
> Bending her neck she licks the tender young,
> And quiet, shapes their bodies with her tongue.
> Not far from this, *Rome*, &c,   O1

Or from these of *Silius Italicus*, describing the Shield of *Flaminius*, a *Roman* Consul;

> *Tum clypeum quatit, aspersum quem cædibus olim*
> *Celticus ornârat cruor : humentique sub antro,*
> *Ceu fœtum, lupa permulcens puerilia membra*
> *Ingentem Assarici cælo nutribat alumnum.*

> Next, he assumes his Shield, where they behold
> The stains of *Celtick* blood, which he before
> In Battel shed : and, in it carv'd, he bore
> A She-Wolf's Figure, in her gloomy Den,
> Licking a Child's soft Limbs, as it had been
> Her Whelp, and nurs'd of the *Assarick* Line
> A Stem, that afterwards was made Divine.

Mr. ROSS.

The other, from these Verses of *Moschus*, where he describes the Basket of *Europa*,

> Ἀργύρεος μὲν ἔην Νεῖλος ἵνα· ἡ δ' ἄρα χρυσὶς
> Χαλκίη, χρυσὶ δὲ τετυγμένος αὐτὸς ἔην Ζεύς.

> In Silver *Nilus* stood, the *Cow* in Brass,
> And *Jupiter* in Gold engraven was.

The *Fable* presented in the Shield of *Europe* is this. *Europa*, Daughter of *Agenor*, gathering Flowers near the Sea-side, was carryed away by *Jupiter*, in the Form of a Bull, into *Crete*, where she became his Spouse ; by whose Name he caused that part of the World to be called, according to this of *Manilius* [1],

[1] *Astronm. Lib. iv.*

> *Quod superest Europa tenet, quæ prima natantem*
> *Fluctibus excepitque* Jovem, *Taurûmque resolvit.*
> *Ille puellari donavit nomine fluctus,*
> *Et monumenta suâ titulo sacravit amoris.*

Europa

> *Europa* laſt place held, whom *Jove* his Prize
> Through Billows bearing, caſt his Bull's diſguiſe,
> And gave that Sea, to her eternal Fame,
> In memory of his Love, the Virgin's Name.

This Virgin was generally reputed a *Tyrian*. EURIPIDES,

Φοινικογενῆς σαῖ ἡ Τυελας
Τὶκτον Ἐυρώπης ————

SENECA the *Tragedian*,

    Tyriæ per undas vector Europæ nitet :

    Through Waves *Tyrian Europa*'s bearer ſhone.

And *Herodotus* [†] conjectures this quarter of the World was named ἀπ᾽ ἡ Ευελας Ἐυρώπης (which *Valla* renders, *ab* Europa *Tyria*) in his firſt Book, affirming, the *Cretans* ſail'd to *Tyre*, and ſtole her from thence. The *Chronographers*, that follow *Euſebius*, rank this about the time of *Joſhuah*, but the *Arundelian* Marbles (ſet forth by Mr. *Selden*) ſhew, that *Cadmus* came to *Thebes*, and built *Cadmea* at the ſame time, when *Amphictyon* reign'd in *Athens*, which was before the *Iſraelites* forſook *Egypt*. By this it is apparent, that *Europa* was not of *Tyre* ; for that was built long after, viz. according to *Joſephus* [*], before the Temple of *Solomon*, which was begun in the 480. Year after the *Iſraelites* departure out of *Egypt*. It is ſuppoſed, that that part of the *Fable*, which ſeigns her carried away by a Bull, ſignifies no more, then that ſhe was tranſported by Sea in a Ship called the *Bull*, from the Figure of a Bull on the Prow of it.   So LYCOPHRON,

    Ἐι ταυρομόρφω τράμαπῷ μορϱόμμζι

it being among the Ancients the uſual Cuſtom to nominate their Ships from the Ἐπίσημον, or *Inſigne* on the Prow, as the *Tiger*, *Centaure*, and *Triton*, in the Navy of *Æneas*, mention'd by VIRGIL [‡],

    Maſsicus ærata princeps ſecat æquora Tigri.

    I'th' Brazen *Tigre Maſsicus* firſt ſtands.

Filius

Filius æquales comitatus classe catervas
Ingentem remis Centaurum *promovet.——*
Hunc vehit immanis Triton, *& cærula conchâ*
Exterrens freta.————————

His Son attended with an equal Troop
Brings, with tuff Oars, the mighty *Centaure* up.
This mighty *Triton* bore, frighting the Tides
With his fhrill Trump.——

We fhall not need give any further account of this *Fable*, but leave
the further Relation of it to this Poem of *Mofchus*,

Ευρώπη ποτέ Κύπρις ἐπὶ γλυκὺν ἧκεν ὄναρον,
Νυκτὸς ὅτε τρίτατον λάχος ἵσταται, ἐγγύθι δ᾽ ἠώς, &c.

A fweet Dream *Venus* once *Europa* lent,
In Nights third quarter, near the Morns afcent;
Whilft Slumber which her eye-lids fweetly crown'd,
Her Limbs unti'd, and her Eyes foftly bound
(That time which doth all truer Dreams beget.)
Europa Phœnix-child, a Virgin yet,
Alone in a high Chamber taking reft,
Beholds two Countries that for her conteft,
The *Afian*, and her oppofite; both feem'd
Like Women; that a ftranger, this efteem'd
A Native who (a Mother like) doth plead
That fhe of her was born, by her was bred;
The other violent hands upon her laid,
And drew by force the unrefifting Maid,
Urging fhe was as prize to *Jove* defign'd:
Out of the bed fhe ftarts with troubled mind:
And panting heart; the Dream to life's fo near:
Long fate fhe filent; long both Women were

                                              After

After she wak'd presented to her sense,
Till thus at length she breaks her deep suspence.

   Which of the Gods, as now I did repose,
Perplex'd my Fancy with delusive Shows?
My calmer Sleeps disquieting with fear :
What Stranger in my Slumber did appear?
Her love shot suddainly into my Breast
And kindness, like a Mother, she expres'd.
The Gods vouchsafe this Dream a good event!

   She rose, and for her lov'd Companions sent,
In Years, and Friendship, equal, nobly born,
With them for Balls she us'd her self t'adorn;
Or in *Anaurus* current Bathes, with them,
She plucks the fragrant Lilly from her Stem
These straight come to her; each a Basket held
To gather Flowers; so walk they to a Field
Neighb'ring the Sea, whither they often went
Pleas'd with the Waters noise, and Roses scent.

   A Golden Basket fair *Europa* bare,
Rich, yet in *Vulcan*'s Workmanship more rare,
Which *Neptune* first to *Lybia* gave, when he
Obtain'd her Bed, to *Telephassa* she
Wife to her Son, from *Telephassa* last
This to unwed *Europe* her Daughter past
Which many Figures neatly wrought did hold.
Inachian Io was here carv'd in Gold,
Not yet in Woman's shape, but like a Cow,
Who seem'd to swim, and force (enraged) through
The Briny Sea her way; the Sea was Blew;
Upon the highest point of Land to view
The Wave-dividing Heifer, two Men stand;
Jove strokes the wet Cow with his sacred hand,

         M   Who

Who, unto seven-mouth'd *Nilus* crossing over,
Did cast her Horns, and Woman's shape recover,
In Silver *Nilus* Flood, the Cow in Brass,
And *Jupiter* in Gold engraven was ;
Mercury figur'd on the furthest round,
And next him lies distended on the ground
Argos, endu'd with many watchful Eyes,
Out of whose Purple Blood a Bird doth rise,
Proud of his various Flowry Plumes, his Tail
He spreadeth like a swift Ship under Sail,
And comprehends the Border with his Wings ;
Such is the Basket fair *Europa* brings.

   All at the Painted Field arive, where these
With sev'ral Flow'rs their several Fancies please,
One sweet *Narcissus* plucks, another gets
Wilde Savory, Hyacinths, and Violets,
Many faln Spring-born Flow'rs the ground doth share,
Some strive which yellow *Crocus* fragrant Hair
Should faster pluck ; i'th' midst the Queen doth stand
Gathering the Roses Beauty with her hand ;
The Graces so by *Venus* are out-shin'd.
Nor must she long with Flowers divert her mind,
Nor long preserve unstain'd her Virgin Zone,
For *Jove*, upon the Meadow looking down,
By *Venus* subtle Darts was struck in love,
Venus hath power to captivate great *Jove*.
Who of frow'rd *Juno's* jealousie afraid,
And that he might deceive the tender Maid,
In a *Bull's* Shape his Deity doth vail,
Not such as are in Stables bred, or trail
The crooked Plough, the furrow'd Earth to wound,
Or run amongst the Heards in Pasture Ground,

                                        Or

Or are to draw the laden Waggon us'd,
Yellow o're all his body is diffus'd,
Save a white Circle ſhines amidſt his Brow,
His brighter Eyes with amorous Sparkles glow.
His Horns with equal length riſe from his Head,
Like the Moon's Orb, to half a Circle ſpread.

Into the Mead he comes, nor (ſeen) doth fright ;
The Virgins to approach him all delight,
And ſtroke the lovely Bull, whoſe divine ſmell
Doth far the Meads perfumed Breath excel :
Before unblam'd *Europa*'s Feet he ſtood,
Licking her Neck, and the Maid kindly woo'd :
She ſtroak'd, and kiſs'd him ; and the Foam, that lay
Upon his Lip, wip'd with her hand away :
He ſoftly bellow'd, ſuch an humming ſound
Forth breathing, as *Mygdonian* Pipes reſound.
Down at her Feet he kneels, viewing the Maid
With writhed Neck, and his broad Back diſplai'd,
When ſhe to th'fair-haird Virgins thus doth ſay ;
Come hither dear Companions, let us play,
Securely with this Bull, and without fear ;
Who, like a Ship, all on his Back will bear.
He tame appears to ſight, and gently kind,
Diff'ring from others, a diſcurſive mind
Bearing like Men, and onely Voice doth lack.

This ſaid, ſhe ſmiling gets upon his Back ;
Which the reſt off'ring, the Bull leaps away,
And to the Sea bears his deſired Prey ;
She cals with ſtretch'd-out hands, ſhe turns to view
Her Friends, alaſs unable to purſue ;
Down leaps he, *Dolphin*-like glides through the Seas :
Up from the Deep riſe the *Nereides*,

M 2　　　　　　　　Mounted

Mounted on Whales to meet her on the way :
Whilst hollow-founding *Neptune* doth allay
The Waves, and is himself his Brothers guide
In this Sea-Voyage ; *Tritons*, on each fide,
(The Deep's inhabitants) about him throng,
And found with their long fhels a nuptial fong ;
She by transformed *Jupiter* thus born,
With one hand holding faft the Bull's large Horn
Her purple garment with the other faves
Unwet by the fwoln Ocean's froathy waves :
Her mantle (flowing o're her fhoulders, fwell'd
Like a full fail, and the young maid upheld.
Now born away far from her native coaft,
Her fight the wave-wafht fhore and mountains loft.
She fees the Heav'ns above, the Seas beneathe,
And, looking round about, thefe Cries doth breathe.
  O whither facred Bull? who art thou, fay?
That through undreaded floods canft break thy way :
The Seas are pervious to fwift Ships alone,
But not to Bulls is their fear'd voyage known ;
What food is here? or if fome God thou be
Why doft, what misbefeems a Deity?
Upon the Land no Dolphins, no Bulls move
Upon the Sea ; Thou Sea and Land doft prove
Alike ; whofe feet like Oares afsift thy haft ;
Perhaps thou'lt foar through the bright Air at laft
On high, and like the nimble Birds become.
Me moft unhappy, who have left my home,
A Bull to follow, voyages unknown
To undertake, and wander all alone.
But *Neptune* thou , that rul'ft the foaming Main
Be pleas'd to help me ; fure I fhall obtain

                                        A

A ſight of this great God, who is my guide,
Nor elſe could I theſe fluid paths have tride.
  The largely horned Bull thus anſwer'd; Maid
Be bold, nor of the ſwelling waves afraid,
For I am *Jove* who now a Bull appear,
And whatſoever ſhape I pleaſe can wear;
In this to meaſure the wide Sea conſtrain'd
For love of thee, thou ſhalt be entertain'd
By *Creet* my Nurſe; our Nuptials ſhall be there
Perform'd, and thou of me great Sons ſhalt bear,
To whoſe imperious Scepters all ſhall bow.
  What he had ſaid, event made good; *Creet* now
Appears in view; *Jove* his own form doth take,
And loos'd her Zone; the Hours their Bed did make,
She late a Virgin, Spouſe to *Jove* became,
Brought him forth Sons, and gain'd a Mothers name.

Mr. STANLEY.

" ASIA, *On her Head a Glory, her Stole of Silk, with ſeveral Forms*
"*of Wild Beaſts wrought on it.*

Among the Poets, we frequently find *Aſia* called *Aurora*, from the
riſing of the Sun there: as in CLAUDIAN,

Jam Princeps molitur iter, gentésque remotas
Colligit Auroræ, *tumidus quaſcunque pererrat*
Euphrates, *quos luſtrat* Halys, *quos ditat* Orontes, &c.

The Prince his Progreſs now deſigning calls
Remoteſt Eaſtern Nations, they whoſe Walls
Euphrates, Halys, and *Oront* improves,
The *Arabs* leave their Incenſe-bearing Groves, &c.

—— *Totam pater undique ſecum*
Moverat Auroram: miſtis hic Colchus Iberis,

Hic mitrâ velatus Arabs, *hic crine decoro*
Armenius.———

——— the Eastern World he rais'd :
There with *Iberians Colchians* mix'd, and there
Wilde *Arabs,* and fair-hair'd *Armenians* were.

And speaking of *Asia,* going to sollicite *Stilico* for Assistance,

Tendit ad Italiam *supplex* Aurora *potentem.*

To *Italy Aurora* supplyant bends.

From whence they represented her like the Rising Sun.   *Claudian* implicitely delivers her ordinary Dress, though in regard of her calamity, at that time, in mourning,

Non radiis redimita comam, nec flammea vultum,
Nec croceum vestita diem ; stat livida luĉta.

No Raies, nor Glory dress'd her Brows, nor clad
In Purple day, but pale she look'd, and sad.

Her Mantle of Silk speaks her ancient Propriety in it : which came so late into *Europe,* that we finde no name for it in *Homer,* among his so frequent Descriptions of the Vestments both of Gods, and Men. **Nay,** not in the Poets of the Old, or Middle Comedy , some hundreds of Years after *Homer.* Whence we conjecture, it was first brought into *Europe* after the Conquest of *Alexander* the Great. After it was brought over, the *Europæans* seem to have had no certain knowledge how it was made. For, by what we can finde, they thought it to have grown naturally on the Trunk, or Leaves of some Trees in *Asia.* So *Virgil,*

Quid nemora Æthiopum *molli canentia lanâ,*
Velleráque ut foliis depeĉtant tenuia Seres?

Of Trees in *Æthiopia* white with Wool ;
How from the Leaves the *Seres* Fleeces cull?

PLINY,

PLINY, *The* Seres *are the firſt, who are known to have a Woolly ſub-*
ſtance to grow on their Trees, which they comb off after they have ſprinkled it
with Water. And *Julius Pollux* * ſpeaks it as a report of ſome, that the
Seres gathered their Silk from certain Worms, like unto the *Bombyces*
of the Iſland *Coos.* Whence it appears, that in the time of *Commodus*
the Emperour, in whoſe time *Pollux* wrote, it was generally believed to
have been otherwiſe : and after that too, for *Claudian,* who flouriſh'd
under the Emperour *Honorius,* agrees with *Pliny ;*

———————— *& pollice docto*
Jam parat auratas trabeas, currusque micantes
Stamine, quod molli tondent de ſtipite Seres,
Frondea lanigeræ carpentes vellera Sylvæ.

——————————— ſhe rarely taught,
Rich Robes prepar'd, and Golden Chariots wrought,
With Thred, which from the Bark the *Seres* cull,
Shearing from ſpreading Boughs the Fleeey Wooll.

Servius indeed, who lived in the time of *Theodoſius,* as appears by his
being cotemporary with † *Macrobius,* had a right opinion of it, as
appears from theſe words of his in the fore-cited place of *Virgil,*
Amongſt the Indians, *and* Seres, *are certain Worms upon the Trees, which*
are called Bombyces; *which, like Spiders, ſpin a very fine Thred, from*
whence is made Silk.
　In the time of *Juſtinian* * the whole Myſtery was diſclos'd by ſome
Monks, who brought from the *Indies* ſome of the Eggs of the Worms :
Since which time that Manufacture ha's been conſtantly uſed in *Eu-*
rope.
　That ſhe ha's ſeveral Shapes, or Forms of ſtrange Beaſts wrought
on her Veſt, is agreeable to the ancient Cuſtoms of that Countrey,
Ariſtophanes †,

'Ουχ ἱππαλεϰθρυόνας, οὐϊε Ϯϱαγελάφϗς, ᾗπῳ σὺ,
'Α ᾿ τοῖσι ϖαϱαπετάσμασι τοῖς Μηδιϰοῖς γϱάφϗσι·

Myne not like your Prodigious Monſters *be,*
Such as are wrought in Median *Tapeſtry.*

　　　　　　　　　　　　　　　　　　PETRONIUS

PETRONIUS ARBITER,

Tuo palato clausus pavo pascitur,
Plumato amictus auleo Babylonico.

A Peacock shall be cram'd for thee,
Adorn'd like *Median* Tapestry.

SIDONIUS,

Peregrina det supellex
Ctesiphontis ac Niphatis
Juga texta belluásque
Rapidas vacante panno
Acuit quibus furorem
Bene scita plaga cocco
Jaculoque ceu forante
Cruor incruentus exit :
Ubi torvus, & per artem
Resupina flexus ora,
It equo redítque telo
Fugiens fugánsque Parthus.

From *Ctesiphont* straight get enough,
And *Niphates* fair Houshold stuff,
Wrought with Hills, and Wilde Beasts, which
The empty Prospect may enrich ;
Who by well-feign'd Wounds enrag'd,
Seem more desperately engag'd,
From *Javelins* fixed in their sides,
Blood in Bloodless Rivers glides ;
Where the *Parthian* with such Art,
O're his Shoulder throws his Dart :
His Horse now charging, then retreats,
And flying, so his Foe defeats.

"AFRICA

"AFRICA, a Woman, in her Hand a Pomegranate; on her Head a
"Crown of Ivory, and Ears of Wheat; at her Feet two Ships laden
"with Corn.

Thus we finde the Statue of *Africk* at *Florence* leaning upon its left
Hand, in which there is a Pomegranate; in her right Hand an *Um-
brella*, to defend her from the heat of the Sun; for her Pillow, two
great Waters, signifying the *Mediterranean*, and *Atlantick* Seas. So
at *Mycenæ*, the Statue of *Juno* (Protectrice of *Carthage*, the Metropolis
of *Africk*) made by *Polyclet*, holds in one Hand a Scepter; in the other,
a Pomegranate. Therefore, when the Queen sacrificed to *Juno*, she
wore a Rod of Pomegranate upon her Head, called by the Ancients
Inarculum. FESTUS; *Inarculum virgulta erat ex malo Punico incur-
vata, quam Regina sacrificans in capite gestabat.*

She is crowned with Ears of Corn, to signifie the Fertility of the
place. *Horace,*

> *Fulgentem imperio fertilis* Africæ
> *Fallit forte beatior.*

> Thou happier art, then he commands
> Rich *Africk*'s fertile Strands.

Thus SIDONIUS introduces *Africa,*

> *Jam malè fœcundas in vertice fregit aristas,*
> *Et sic orsa loqui est.*

> Her Wheat-ear'd Wreath now early full she broke,
> And thus then spoke.

And CLAUDIAN,

> *Tum spicis, & dente comas illustris eburno,*
> *Et valido rubicunda die, sic* Africa *satur.*

> With Iv'ry crown'd, and Wheat, red with the Sun,
> And fainting Heats, thus *Africa* begun.

N   According

According to which Defcription of his , we finde her reprefented in a
Coyn of *Antoninus Pius*,

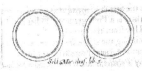

Seld. Mar. Aruf. bb. 5.

De Bello
Gildonico.

The fame Authour implicitely defcribes her, in the fame manner, in
another place,

—————— *mediis apparet in aftris*
Africa, refciffæ veftes, & Spicea paßim
Serta jacent, lacero crinales vertice dentes,
Et fractum pendebat ebur. ——————

Amidft the Stars next *Africa* appears
Her Garments torn, her Wreath of Wheaten Ears
Scatter'd about, Teeth braided on her Crown,
And broken Ivory hung.——————

Plin. Nat.
Hift. vii. 51.

The Ivory on her Head, alludes to the great number of Elephants,
bred in that part of the World ; efpecially in that *part of* Africa *beyond*
the Syrtick *Solitudes, and Defarts*, Æthiopia, Troglodicica, *and* Mauri-
tania. *Petronius,*

Quæritur in filvis Mauri fera ; & ultimus Ammon
Afrorum excutitur, nè defit bellua dente
Ad mortes pretiofa fuas. ——————

The *Libyan* Wilds we feek, and th'utmoft South,
To finde a Monfter out, whofe pretious Tooth
Proves its own bane.——————

JUVENAL.

JUVENAL,

Dentibus ex illis quos mittit porta Syenes,
Et Mauri *celeres.* ——————

From whiter Teeth, which the *Syene* ſends,
And the ſwift *Moors.*——————

Whence the *Romans*, in their Triumphs over *Africa*, uſually had Elephants led before them, to denote the place of their Victory : as *L.*
Metellus, in whoſe Coyns we finde either an Elephant, or his Triumphal Chariot drawn by two of them, or a Head of one of them under
his Chariot.

Plin. lib. viii. cap. vii.

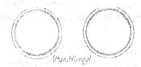

(Aer. Morell.)

Pliny ſays, that the Chariot of *Pompey* was drawn by four Elephants in his *African* Triumph. And we finde that the Fifth Legion
bore the Effigies of an Elephant on their Colours , becauſe they ſuc-
ceſsfully manag'd a Battel againſt them, in the War betwixt *Cæſar*, and
L. Scipio.

Lib. lxi. cap. vi.

The two Ships at her Feet, relate to the *Claſſis Frumentaria*, which
came yearly to *Rome* from *Africk* : frequently mention'd in the *Ro-*
man Writers; which was inſtituted by *Commodus* the Emperour. Of
whom *Lampridius* ; *Claſſem* Africanam *inſtituit quæ ſubſidio eſſet, ſi forte*
Alexandrina *frumenta ceſſaſſent.* He appointed an *African* Navy,
which ſhould furniſh the City , in caſe the Corn from *Alexandria*
ſhould fail. Of which *Claudian*,

Tot mihi pro meritis Libyam Nilumque dedére,
Ut dominam plebem bellatoremque Senatum
Claſſibus æſtivis alerent, geminóque viciſſim
Littore diverſi complerent horrea venti.

De Bello Gildon.

N 2

Stabat

Stabat certa ſalus : Memphis ſi fortè negaſſet,
Penſabam Pharium Getulis meſſibus annum.
Frugiferas certare rates, latéque videbam
Punica Niliacis concurrere carboſa velis.

They gave me *Libya,* and the *Ægyptian* Shore
For my deſerts, that they might with their Store
·The People, and the Warlick Senate feed,
And with contrary Winds ſupply their need.
Famine farewel : if *Memphis* ſhould deny,
Getulian Harveſts will our Wants ſupply.
Freighted with Corn, I ſaw the *Punick* Fleet,
And Ships from *Nilus* in our Harbours meet.

And,

Lende Stri-
na Rig 106.

——*Phariæ ſegetes & * Punica meſſis
          Caſtrorum devota cibo : dat Gallia *robur*
          Militis, &c. ——

—— *Ægyptian Crops, and* Punick *Grain*
          Our Camps with Bread, Gaul *doth with Men maintain.*

De Provi-
dentia Dei,
Lib. VI.
Wherefore *Salvian,* after he had mention'd the Deſtruction of *Sardi-*
nia, and *Sicily,* the Vital Veins, he calls *Africa* the Soul it ſelf of the
Common-Wealth of *Rome. Prudentius,*

In Sym-
machuus.

          Reſpice num Libyci *deſiſtat raris arator*
          Frumentis onerare rates, & ad Oſtia Tibris
          Mittere triticeos in paſtum plebis acervos.

See if the *Libyan* Swain negleдts to load
Our Ships with Corn, and to the *Oſtian* Road
Sends Wheaten Mountains for the Peoples Food.

" A M E R I C A *Crown'd with Feathers of divers Colours, on her Stole a*
" *Golden River, in one Hand a Silver Mountain.*

                                                            So

So *Pompey*, in his Triumph over *Methridates*, among the rest of his Silver and Golden Representations carried *Montem aureum, quadratum, cum cervis & leonibus, & pomis omnis generis, circumdatâ vite aureâ, A square Golden Mountain, encompassed with a Vine of Gold, with Harts and Lions upon it, and all manner of Fruit.* The Mountain in her Hand is *Potosi* in *Peru,* whose Treasure ha's been accounted inexhaustible. *Josephus Acosta* relates, that in that Mountain there was found a Vein of Silver, about the height of a Spear above the Superficies of the Earth, three hundred Foot long, and thirteen broad. The same Authour witnesses, that the King of *Spain* receives yearly from thence a Million of Ducats; and that onely from the fifth part of the Silver. We have read of indeed of Silver Mountains in *Europe*; as that mention'd by *Strabo* in *Spain*; *Not far from* Costaon *is a Mountain, whence flows the River* Bætis, *call'd the* Silver Mountain, *in relation to the Silver Mines there.* And of a Golden Mountain in *Asia,* mention'd by *Menander*; ἵνα ὁ Χαγάνϑ αὐτὸς ἦν, ἐν ᾧ ἐςι τὴι Διρμαίρν Ἐκ]ὰγ (presently after Ἐκ]ὰγ) ὅς ἀι εἶποι, χρεσόμ ᾿ϕϐ᾿ Ἐκάλω ἀύϕ, *Where King* Chaganus *himself was, on a Mountain call'd* Ectag, *that is, the* Golden Mountain. And *Appian* before him; *Many Fountains bring down small Shavings of Gold from the Mountain* Caucasus; *the Inhabitants sinking Fleeces of Woollvery deep, take up what Shavings stick to them* : But these are all so considerable, in respect of the inestimable Treasure of this Mountain, that *America* may reasonably from hence, as all other Countries from what is most valuable, and appropriate to them, have its distinguishing Character.

The River on her Stole is the Golden River *Peru.* So *Claudian* represents *Brittain* with the Flux and Deflux of the Sea on her Vest;

> *Inde Caledonio velata* Britannia *monstro,*
>
> *Ferro pictâ genas, cujus vestigia verrit*
>
> *Cærulus, Oceanique æstum mentitus amictus,*

> *Britannia* then veil'd in a Boars rough Hide,
>
> Walk'd on the Sea, her Cheeks with Iron dy'd,
>
> Cloath'd with the changings of the Oceans Tide.

And S P A I N, with the Golden River *Tagus* on her Stole :

> —— *glaucis tum prima* Minervæ
>
> *Nexa comam foliis, fulváque intexta micantem*
>
> *Veste* Tagum, *tales profert* Hispania *voces.*

Then

Then *Spain* with Olive-Branches crown'd, her Veſt
With Golden *Tagus* wrought, her ſelf expreſt
In words like theſe. ―――――

Mag. claſſ.
Lib. ii. Which Leaves of *Minerva*, Mr. *Selden* miſtook for a Palm. *Claudian*,
in ſeveral places, deſcribes the Olive in the ſame manner ; as in his Epiſtle to *Hadrian*,

> *Hoc pro ſupplicibus ramis, pro fronde* Minervæ,
> *Hoc carmen pro thure damus.* ―――――

> This for *Minerva's* ſupplicating Bough,
> This Verſe for Incenſe we beſtow.

And in another place,

In Eutrop.
Poet, Lib. ii. > ―――――― *pro fronde* Minervæ
> *Has tibi protendo lacrymas.* ――――

> ――――― for *Pallas* Boughs,
> Theſe Tears we thee preſent,

LUCAN,

De Bell.
Civ. lib. iii. > ――――――― *tamen ante furorem*
> *Indomitum, duramque viri deflectere mentem*
> *Pacifico Sermone parant, hostemque propinquum*
> *Orant* Cecropiæ *prælatâ fronde* Minervæ.

> ――――――― they to aſſwage
> His cruel Breaſt, accuſtomed to rage,
> *Minerva's* Branches ſtretching forth, beſeech
> The Neighb'ring Foe with a prepared Speech.

In which places 'tis evident, the Olive is ſignified, becauſe carried in
the Hands of Suppliants. *Statius*,

> ―――― *ramumque precantis Olivæ.*
> A ſupplicating Olive Branch.

Vittatæ

Vittatæ laurus, & supplicis arbor Olivæ.

With Bays and supplicating Olives crown'd.

Whence *Virgil* makes *Æneas* send a hundred to King *Latinus*, all crown'd with Olive Branches, call'd there *Palladis rami.*

———— *ramis velatos* Palladis *omnes,*
Donaque ferre viro, pacemque expofcere Teucris.

And for the *Trojans* Terms of Peace propound,
With Royal Prefents, all with Olive crown'd.

And *Statius* makes *Tydeus,* going in the name of *Polynices,* to demand the Kingdom of *Thebes,* carry a Branch of Olive in his Hand, as a token of Peace ; and, his Demand being denied, to throw away the fame, to fignifie, and declare a War. So LIVY, *Not far off was a Ship of the* Carthaginians, *covered with Mitres, and Branches of Olive ; in which were ten Ambaffadours, chief Princes of the City, fent to requeft Peace.*

CLAUDIAN gives the fame Epithet too, to the Olive-leaves, in his Epiftle to SERENA,

———— *glaucâ pinguis Oliva comâ.*

The unctuous Olive with a Silver Sprig.

And VALERIUS FLACCUS,

———— *glaucásque comis prætexere frondes Imperat.*

Commands to braid their Hair with verdant Boughs.

The reafon why *Claudian* fo defcribes it, is, becaufe that Tree was facred to *Minerva:* which we finde attefted by *Pliny; The Efculus* (a Species of glandiferous Trees) *is facred to* Jupiter ; *the Laurel to* Apollo, *the Olive to* Minerva, *the Myrtle to* Venus, *the Poplar to* Hercules ; and is known from the Fable of the Contention of *Minerva,* and *Neptune,* concerning the Poffeffion of *Athens.* And *Epopeus,* after a Victory, having erected and confecrated to her a Temple, and pray'd, that fhe would fhow fome token of her acceptance of it, there prefently fprung forth a Branch of Olive before it.

This

Argonaut.
Lib. iii.

Nat. Hiſt.
lib. xii. c. i.

Pauſan.
lib. ii.

This Errour of Mr. *Selden*'s produc'd another in his following words, when he gather'd from thence, that the River *Tagus*, and Palm-Trees were proper to *Spain*. Hispaniæ *Palmæ, & *Tagus *fluvius propria*. Indeed the Palm-Tree was the Symbol of *Judæa*, as we see in the Coyns of *Vespasian* and *Titus*,

from the abundance of them in that Countrey. STRABO: *Beside the common Palm, it* (Judæa) *brings forth the* Carupta, *not much inferiour to the* Babylonian. *Lucan*,

> ——*Et arbusto Palmarum dives* Idume,

And *Idumea* rich with Palm.

Lib. iii. SILIUS ITALICUS,

> *Palmiferámque senex bello domitabit* Idumen,

Palm-bearing *Idumæa* shall subdue.

But *Spain* was commended for the abundance, and excellency of its Olives. *Martial*,
Epigram. Lib. xii.

> Bætis, *Olivifer'à crinem redimite coronâ,*
> *Aurea qui nitidis vellera tingis aquis.*

> *Bætis* her Tresses crown'd with Olive Stems,
> Dyes Golden Fleeces with her glitt'ring Streams.

Lib. iii. Which Verses, compared with these of *Silius Italicus*, evidently evince, that *Palladis rami* signifie the Olive.

> ————*genuit quos ubere ripâ*
> *Palladio* Bethes *umbratus cornua ramo.*

—both

——— both of equal age
Born upon *Bethes* Banks, whoſe horned Brows
Were overſhadowed with fat Olive Boughs,

And in another place, of *Spain*,   I.I.I.

> *Nec* Cereri *terra indocilis, nec inhoſpita* Baccho,
> *Nulláque* Palladiâ *ſeſe magis arbore tollit.*

A Land, where *Ceres*, and *Lyæus* too
Do dwell, and Olive-Trees in plenty grow.

Whence, in a Coyn of *Hadrian* the Emperour, we finde that Coun-
trey ſignified by a Woman ſitting, with her left hand leaning on the
Pyrenean Mountains (Mr. *Selden* calls it a heap of Stones) in her right
Hand holding a Branch of Olive ; at her Feet a Coney :

Croyſac.
Tab.xxxii.

The Coney we finde too at the Feet of *Spain*, holding an Olive-
Branch on her Shoulder, in a Coyn of the ſame Emperour.

Ibid.

The Coney at her Feet ſignifies either the incredible number of
thoſe Animals formerly in *Spain* (for *Varro* mentions a Town there
                                    undermin'd

O

Lib.xlii.cap.
XXII.

undermin'd, and overthrown by them, as we finde in *Pliny*) or rather the abundance of Mines in that Countrey; the *Latine* word *Cu-*
niculi, from whence the allusion must be taken, being æquivocal, and an-
swering to both. From one of which significations a part of *Spain* is
call'd *Cuniculosa Celtiberia* by *Catullus*,

Epigram.
XXXV.

> *Tu præter omnes, une de capillatis,*
> *Cuniculosæ* Celtiberiæ *fili.*

The Mines are mentioned by *Claudian*, speaking of *Spain*,

> *Dives equis, frugum facilis, pretiosa metallis,*
> *Principibus fæcunda piis.* ———

> With Steeds abounding, rich with **Corn, and Ore,**
> And pious Princes store. ——

De Bello
Pun. lib. 1.

And by SILIUS ITALICUS,

> ——— *hic omne metallum :*
> *Electri gemino pallent de semine venæ,*
> *Atque atros chalybis fœtus humus horrida nutrit.*
> *Sed scelerum causas aperit Deus. Astur avarus*
> *Visceribus laceræ telluris mergitur imis,*
> *Et redit infelix effosso concolor auro.*

> ——— here Metals grow
> Of matter mix'd : *Electrum's* pallid **Veins**
> Produc'd, and darker Steel the Earth contains :
> But God those Springs of mischief deeply **hides** ;
> Yet *Astur*, covetous, the Earth divides,
> And, in her mangled Entrails drown'd **again,**
> Returns with Gold, and bears the pretious Stain.

But

But to return. This River, says *Jofephus Acofta*, gave the name to
the whole Countrey of *Peru*. Of which *Levinus Apollonius* thus, under another name; where he defcribes the Rivers of the Mountainous P E R U, *The chiefeft far is the River* Argyreus (P E R U) *from
its abundance of Silver, which it cafts up in glittering Sand, call'd in* Spanifh,
Plata: *it is equally liberal, and profufe of its Treafure unto all parts it
paffeth by, enriching its Inhabitants with an inexhauftible abundance both of
Gold, and Silver.*

*Hift. Nat.
Ind.* lib. i.
cap. xiii.

*De Peruviæ
regionib: ur-
ountibe.*

"*The uppermoft great* Table *in the fore-ground reprefents* King
"Charles the Firft, with the Prince, *now* Charles the Second, *in His
"Hand, viewing the Sovereign of the Sea, the Prince leaning on a Can-
"non; the Infcription,*

O NIMIUM DILECTE DEO, CUI MILITAT
ÆQUOR,
ET CONJURATI VENIUNT AD CLASSICA
VENTI.

For thee, O *Jove's* Delight, the Seas engage,
And muftr'ed Winds, drawn up in Battel, rage.

"*Above, over the* Cornich, *between the two* Celeftial *Hemi-fpheres,
"an* Atlas, *bearing a* Terreftrial *Globe, and on it a* Ship *under Sail; the
"Word,*

UNUS NON SUFFICIT.

Thus we finde *Atlas* painted in an ancient Temple of *Jupiter's.*
PAUSANIAS, *Amongft the reft, is the Picture of* Atlas, *bearing up Heaven,
and Earth; by whom ftands* Hercules, *as ready to affift him:* mention'd
by *Claudian,*

In Eliacis.

————*fic,* Hercule *quondam
Suftentante polum, melius librata pependit
Machina, nec dubiis titubavit Signifer aftris.
Perpetuàque fenex fubductus mole parumper
Obftupuit proprii fpectator ponderis* Atlas.

O 2

————fo

──────── ſo *Hercules* of old
Suſtain'd the Pole, bore better on his Back
The poyſed World, and fix'd the Zodiack :
Atlas a while, from his great Burthen free,
Admiring ſtood, the wond'rous Load to ſee.

Of whom thus HOMER,

Ἄγαι]Ἐ ἐυγάτηρ ἐλοβρρνῷῷ, ὅνε ϑαλάσσης
Πλάνα ϐύϑεα εἶδεῖ ἔχει Δἰ τε κίονας αὐτὸς
Μακρὰς ἂι γάῖδε τη, ὁ ὑέρανὶ ἀμφ̀ὸ ἰς ἔχρῃσι.

Daughter of *Atlas*, who both Depth, and Sholes
Of th' Ocean plumbs, and holdeth two long Poles,
That mighty Heaven, and the Earth ſuſtain.

In [Προμ.]　ÆSCHYLUS,
Δεσμ.

──────── ὃς πρὸς ἑσπέρας τόπῳς
Ἔσηκε κίν ὑέρανῦ τε ἡ χϑονὸς
Ὤμοις ἐρεὶδεν, ἄχϑ̀ὸς ὀυκ ἐυάγκαλον.

──────── who near the Weſtern Main
Bears on his Back that Pillar, doth ſuſtain
Both Heaven, and Earth, not eaſie to ſupport.

VIRGIL,

──────── *ubi cœlifer* Atlas
Axem humero torquet ſtellis ardentibus aptum.

──────── where great *Atlas* bears,
Laden with Golden Stars, the glittering Sphears.

He was thus deſcribed from his admirable knowledge in the motions
of the Heavens, and the nature of things here below. PAUSANIAS [*], *In*
which there is a place of ground call'd Poloſus, *where they ſay* Atlas *ſtudied*
the Heavens, and the Earth. DIODORUS SICULUS [†], *They ſay, he* (Atlas)
was excellently ſkill'd in Aſtrology, *and was the firſt, that publiſhed the Sphe-*
rical

[*] *In Bœtiis.*
[†] *L. b. iii.*

rical *Figure of the Heavens* : *from whence he was ſaid to bear the Heavens on his Shoulders* ; *the Fable ſignifying the Invention, and Deſcription of the Sphere*. Which ſeems not be underſtood of a ſolid Sphere, but a Sphere deſcribed on a Plane : the other Invention, by moſt of the Ancients, being attributed to *Archimedes*, who liv'd many Centuries of Years after him.

" *The great Painting on the* Weſt-*ſide repreſents the Duke of* YORK,
" *habited* à l'antique, *like* Neptune, *ſtanding on a Shell drawn by Sea-*
" Horſes, *before which a* Triton *ſounding, in one Hand a* Trident, *the*
" Reins *in the other* ; *his* Motto,

SPES ALTERA.

We generally finde *Neptune* among the Poets drawn by Sea-Horſes. STATIUS,   *Theb.* Lib. ii.

> *Illic* Ægeo Neptunus *gurgite feſſos*
> *In portum deducit equos, prior haurit habenas*
> *Ungula, poſtremi ſolvuntur in æquor a piſces.*

> Here *Neptune* entring left th'*Ægean* Flood,
> Landing his Steeds, their formoſt Feet well ſhod :
> The hindmoſt cut the Waves with Finny Tails.

VIRGIL,   *Æneid.* v.

> *His ubi læta Deæ permulſit pectora dictis,*
> *Jungit equos curru genitor, ſpumantiáque addit*
> *Fræna ferit, manibúsque omnes effundit habenas,*
> *Cæruleo per ſumma levis volat æquora curru.*

> When thus her troubled Breaſt he had aſſwag'd,
> He joyns his Chariot-Horſe, and curbs th'enrag'd
> With Fomy Bits, then gives them lib'ral Rein,
> With blew Wheels flying o're the Azure Main.

They were called *Hippocampæ*. NONIUS; Hippocampæ, *equi marini, à flexu caudarum, quæ piſcoſæ ſunt*. Hippocampæ are Sea-Horſes,

ſo

so called from the flexion of their Tails, which are like Fishes. FESTUS; *Campas marinos equos Græci à flexione posteriorum partium appellant,* "The "*Greeks* call Sea-Horses *Campæ,* from the bending of their posteriour "parts: from καμπειν *to bend.*

In the Medaigles of *Caius Marius,* and *Quintus Creperius,* is represented *Neptune* riding upon these *Hippocampæ,* or Sea-Horses.

Card.Gebr.
in Fasth ad
6.56.

And the Form of a Sea-Horse we have in the Coyn of the Emperour *Gallienus,*

Ciacc.

As he holds the Reins of his Horses in one hand, so we finde him constantly with a Trident in the other. From whence he is call'd by the *Greeks,* τριαινης, ευτριαινα *, τριαινοφρον, by *Pindar* βαρυκτυπον by the *Latines, Tridentifer,* and *Tridentiger.* OVID,

* Pindar
in Crat.
Plutarh.
* Epigr.Gr.
† Metam.
lib. viii

———— *ô proxima terræ*
 Regna vagæ, dixi, sortite Tridentifer undæ.

And,

  Cùmque Tridentigero tumidi genitore profundi.

VIRGIL,

———— *Tuque, O, cui prima frementem*
 Fudit equum magno tellus percussa Tridenti,
Neptune.————

————and

———— and *Neptune*, thou, to whom
The Earth first *Trident* struck brought forth a Steed.

HOMER, *Iliad. μ.*

> Αὐτὸς δ᾽ ἐννοσίγαιΘ ἔχων χείρεσσι τρίαιναν
> Ἡγεῖτ᾽ ἐκ δ᾽ ἄρα πάντα θεμείλια κύμασι πέμπε
> Φιτρῶν, ᾧ λάων.————

> *Arm'd with his Trident*, Neptune, *leading on*
> *Impetuous Waves, left neither Pile, nor Stone.*

Callimachus, singularly, says, that his Trident was made by the *Tel-* *Hymn in* *chines*, smiths in *Creet*. *Delon.*

> ———— ὕρεα θείων
> Ἄοςι τεχνλάχιν, τὸ δι Τελχῖνες ἐτευξαι.

> ———— *Neptune* the Mountain struck
> With's *Trident*, which the *Telechines* made.

Plutarch tells, that the *Trœzenians* mark their Moneys with a Trident, as a Testimony of their Devotion to *Neptune*.

Amongst the rest of *Neptune's* Attendants was *Triton* his Trum-
peter. OVID, *Metam.*

> *Cæruleum* Triton*a vocat, conchâque sonanti*
> *Inspirare jubet, fluctibusque, & flumina signo*
> *Jam revocare dato.*————

> *Triton he calls, commanding him to sound*
> *His hollow Shell, and call the Floods profound,*
> *And Rivers back.* ————

VIRGIL, speaking of a Ship, *Æneid.*

> ———— *Immanis* Triton, & cærula conchâ
> *Exterrens freta. Cui laterum tenùs hispida nanti*
> *Frons hominem præfert ; in Pristin desinit alvus :*
> *Spumea semifero sub pectore murmurat unda.*

This

This mighty *Triton* bore, frighting the Tides
With his shrill Trump. His Face, and hairy sides
Above presents a Man, a Whale the rest :
And foamy Waves resound beneath his Breast.

Imagin.
Lib.xi.
NONNUS,

Τελλων δ' ιυρηιστ᾽ ιδέμβαιν ὸτὰλᾶ νέχλϙ
Ἀνδροφυὴς, ἀπέλιςτ᾽, ἀπ᾽ ἰξῦϙ ὐγχλᾶϙ ἰχθυῖ

Broad-bearded *Triton* sounds his Trump at last,
Half humane Shape, a Fish beneath the Waste.

Idyll.
MOSCHUS,

——— οἱ δ' ἀωφί μιν ἐφρίωντο.
Τελλωτις, πελίγιι βαδνζρὸν ἐναιέτραι,
Κόχλονσι νια ἀ λὸ νὰφαιι μελνὰδ ἐνιάντιν

——— *Tritons* on each side
(The Deep's Inhabitants) about him throng,
And sound with their long Shels a Nuptial Song.

  " *On the four* Niches *within the* Arch *were living Figures, with* Escut-
" cheons, *and* Pendents, *representing* Arithmetick, Geometry, Astro-
" nomy, *and* Navigation.
  " Arithmetick, *a* Woman *habited à l'antique, with her Fingers erect* :
" *upon her* Vestment Lines, *with* Musick Notes *on them : in her* Escut-
" cheon *a* Book *opened, with a* Hand *pointing to the Figures*, I. V. X. L. C. D. M.
" &c. *Under*,

PAR ET IMPAR.

  The holding out of her Fingers erect points out to us that ancient
manner of Supputation, known of old to most Countries in the World,
but now out of use, by the Fingers of both Hands.   This Supputation
was divided into three parts; Digits, Decades, and Compound Numbers.   The Digits comprehend all Numbers under ten, the Decads
comprehend all tens, as 10, 20, 30, 40, 50, 60, 70, 80, 90. the Compound what was made of the other two, as 19, 27, &c. The Digits
first

were expreſs'd by the three laſt Fingers, beginning with the little one. The Decads by the Thumb, either ſingle, or in conjunction with the firſt Finger.   Thus far reacheth the *Arithmetique* of the left Hand; ſo that, removing to the right, the firſt Number is an hundred : *Unius nu-merum, quo geſtu ſignificabantur in ſiniſtra, tranſlatum in dexteram centena conficere.* The Number of a Hundred, by the ſame geſture, is ſigni-fied in the right Hand, that one in the left.   And, *A numero nonageſimo, qui fuit in læva, per unius ſignificationem, transferri in dexteram, & ibi cen-tena conſtitui.* From which kind of *Arithmetique* we muſt underſtand that *Greek* Epigram of *Nicarchus,*

H σπλὴ χρονάμαι Κυτυτ]αεὶς ἡ πολομιᾶ@·
  Γοχία, δὶ ἡ Νέτορ ὑκ ἢν σφαλδιεαΙⓄ·
H σ4Ⓞ ἀσρόποις ἰλάφις πηλίι, ἡ χρὶ λαιῇ
  Γῆγει δευλειᾶαι λόνπει ἀξαμίτι.
Ζάι, ῷ λύνσισι, ῷ ἀρπιτⓄ', ὅλαπ πύμφην,
  Ὅτι με διτάξαι μή τι πάντωδ' ἀλόσι.

Grey-hair'd *Cotyttaris,* that infernal Scold,
Whom *Neſtor* to compare with was not old ;
Whoſe many Years the long-liv'd Harts ſurmount,
She on her left Hand twice begins to count.
Swift-footed as a *Nymph,* her ſight not fails,
Sure, I believe, the Devil ſomething ails.

And this of JUVENAL,

Rex Pylius, magno ſi quidquam credis Homero,
  Exemplum vitæ fuit à Cornice ſecundæ.
Felix nimirum ! qui tot per ſæcula vitam
  Diſtulit, atque ſuos jam dextrâ computat annos.

Neſtor, if thou'lt great *Homer* credit give,
As long as did the long-liv'd Raven live ;
Bleſs'd thou ! who ſtood'ſt ſo many Luſtres rage,
Till on thy right Hand thou did'ſt count thy Age.

So that as the Units were counted on the three Fingers of the left, ſo the firſt Nine Hundred were counted on the ſame three Fingers of the right ;   and as the Decads were counted on the Thumb, and

P

Fore-Finger of the left, so were the Thousands on the same of the right.
Whence we may guess of the Figure of the Fingers, which *Pliny* *
mentions in the Statue of *Janus*, dedicated by *Numa*, with his *Fingers
so complicated, that the Note of* cccLxv *Days, the signification of a Year,
should demonstrate him the God of Time.*

Of this manner of Supputation must be understood that Saying of
Orontes, who, upon some distast taken by King *Artaxerxes*, had fallen into disgrace ; " As the Fingers of Accountants now reprelent one , now
" *Myriads*; so the Friends of Kings now are much in favour, now not at
all. This manner of Supputation seems to have been ordinary among
the *Romans*, used in their Pleadings before the Judge. Quintilian ',
*Si actor, non dice, si circa summas trepidat, sed se digitorum incerto foliam, aut
indecoro gestu à computatione dissentit, judicatur indoctus.* " If the Pleader
" not onely trembles about the Sums, but if by a doubtful onely, and un-
" comely gesture, he differs from the Computation, he is esteemed un-
" learned. *Apuleius* in his Apologetical Oration before Æmilianus, *Si
triginta annos pro decem dixisses, posses videri pro computationis gestu errasse,
quos circulare debueris, digitos aperuisse.* If you had nam'd thirty Years for
*ten, you might seem to have mistaken in the gesture of your Computation, to have
circled those Fingers, which you should have opened.* And therefore it is very
strange, that, after so common an usage of this manner of Computation,
it should be so far lost, that none can agree what it was.

The Authour of *Arithmetique*, according to *Æschylus* ', was *Prometheus*:

Καὶ μὴν ἀριθμὸν ἔξοχον σοφισμάτων
Ἐξεῦρον ἀυτοῖς, γραμμάτων τε συνθέσεις.

The chief of Arts I Numbers found,
And first knew Letters to compound.

According to *Plato*, 'twas *Palamedes*: but *Pliny* * attributes the Invention of it to *Minerva*; *Eóque* Minervæ *Templo dicatam legem, quia nu-
merus à* Minerva *inventus sit.*

The ancient Musick-Notes here mention'd, though for many hundred Years buried in obscurity, have been brought to light again out
of some *Greek* Authours of Musick, lately publish'd by *Meibomius*.
The Numbers are sufficiently known , though not so well as those we
generally use, lately brought into *Europe* from the *Arabians*.

" Geometry

"Geometry, *a Woman in a pleasant* Green, *in her Shield a* Com-
"pass, *and a* Read; *the* Inscription,

DESCRIPSIT RADIO TOTUM QUÆ GENTIBUS
ORBEM.

Geometry is supposed by the Ancients to have had its original in
Ægypt, where, after the yearly overflowings of the River *Nile*, they
were forc'd continually to measure their ground out anew to distin-
guish Propriety. STRABO[†], Καθάπερ ὴ ἡ Ἀιγυπτίων ὥρμα Γεωμετρίας φασὶ,
ἀπὸ ἡ χαρεματείας, ἣν ΝΑ... ἀπεργάζεται, συγχεῖ τὰς ὅρως κατὰ τὰς διαλύσεις. And[*],
ἘΛθόντα δὲ ὁ ἐπ' ἀκριβὲς ἡ μετὰ λαπτὸν διάρεσας διὰ τὰς σωχαχῆς ἡ ὅρων συγχεσις, δὲ ὁ
ΝΑ... ἀπεργάζεται τάλα τὰς ἀυξήσεις ἀφαιρεῖ, ἡ προσθῆκι, ἡ ἀμολίευτα τὰ εγγρατα, ἡ ταῦτα
ἐτερα ἀπεργάσιτα, εἰς διακείνια τὸ τε ἀμόλιεα, ἡ τὸ ὕδαν ἀργύα ἢ ἀπεργάζεται ταῦτα
ἡ τάλα. Ἐπλῦθι δὲ ὁ τῶν Γεωπλεζία συντάξεω φασὶ. For which end, because
they made use of a Read, it was amongst them ever after for a Symbol
of *Geometry*. So in a Silver Coyn of *C. Mamilius*, in one side there is a
Mercury with a Cap, and *Caduceus*, on the other *Mamilius*, with a
Read by him, with this Inscription, L I. METAN. that is, *Limi-
tibus metandis*, where we finde his Office of measuring Land implyed
by a Read.

The Compass in her other Hand we have described by O v i d,

  ——— *& ex uno duo ferrea brachia nodo*
  Junxit, ut æquali spatio distantibus illis
  Altera pars staret, pars altera duceret orbem.

  He two-shank'd Compasses with Rivet bound,
  The one to stand still, th' other turning round,
  In equal distances.——— —

The Authour of it, *Talus*, being envyed by his Uncle *Dædalus* for
this, and other Inventions, was thrown down headlong by him from
the top of *Minerva*'s Tower: but in the middle of his fall, being favour'd
by *Minerva*, the Patroness of Wit, was turn'd into a Bird; which we
have in the following Verses:

  Dædalus *invidit: sacrâque ex arce* Minervæ
  Præcipitem misit, lapsum mentitus: at illum,

Quæ favet ingeniis, excepit Pallas, *avémque*
Reddidit, & medio velavit in aëre pennis.

———————*Dædalus thus began,*
Who from *Minerva's* sacred Turret flung
The envi'd headlong; and his falling fains:
Him *Pallas*, fautor of good Wits, sustains.
Who straight the Figure of a Fowl assumes;
Clad in the midst of Ayr with freckled Plumes.

Mr. SANDYS.

" Astronomy, *a Woman in a loose Vestment*, Azure, *wrought with*
" *Stars of Gold, looking up to Heaven: in her Shield a Table, wherein are*
" *divers* Astronomical *Figures*; *the* Inscription,

AURO CIRCUMSPICIT ORIONA.

ASTRONOMY holding a *Sphere* in her left Hand, in her right a
Radius.
  So she is described by *Martianus Capella.* The Sphere, which he gives
her, is that of *Archimedes*, as we see by the Epigram, in which he describes it,

Ipsa etiam, lævâ, Sphærâ fulgebat honorâ;
  Assimilis mundo, sideribúsque fuit.
Nam globus, & circi, Zonæque, ac fulgida signa
  Nexa recurrebant, arte locata pari.
Tellus, quæ rapidum consistens suscipit orbem,
  Puncti instar medio hæserat una loco.

In her left Hand she a *Celestial* Sphear,
Like the great World, glitt'ring with Stars did bear:
On the vast Globe the circulating Signes
Connexed ran in equidistant Lines

To

To rapid Orbs; the Earth, the fixed Base,
Like a small Point, just in the midst took place.

"Navigation, *a Woman in Sea-green Habit; in her* Escutcheon *an* "Anchor, *with a* Cable *about it; the* Inscription,

TUTUM TE LITTORE SISTAM.

While the *Nobility* passed the *Triumphal Arch*, the three Sea-men entertained them with this Song from the Stage on the *North*-side of the *Arch*.

I.

From Neptune's *Wat'ry Kingdoms, where*
    Storms, and Tempests rise so often,
As would the World in pieces tear,
    Should Providence their Rage not soften;
From that fluctuating Sphere,
    Where stout Ships, and smaller Barks
    Are toss'd like Balls, or feather'd Corks,
    When briny Waves to Mountains swell,
Which dimming oft Heav'n's glitt'ring Sparks,
    Then descending low as Hell;
        Through this Crowd,
        In a Cloud,
By a strange, and unknown Spell,
        We, newly Landing,
        Got this Standing,
All Merry Boys, and Loyal,
        Our Pockets full of Pay,
        This Triumphal Day,
To make of our Skill a Tryal,
    Of our little little Skill:
    Let none then take it ill,
We must have no Denyal.

II.

II.

We, who have rais'd, and laid the Poles,
  Plough'd frozen Seas, and scalding Billows;
Now stiff with Cold, then scorch'd on Coals,
  Ships our Cradles, Decks our Pillows;
'Mongst threatning Rocks, and treach'rous Shoals,
  Through Gibraltar's contracted Mouth,
And 'Realms condemn'd to Heat, and Drowth,
  Or Baltick Waves bound up in Ice,
Or Magellane as Cold, though South,
    Our good Fortune, in a trice,
      Through this Crowd,
      In a Cloud,
Brings us where, in Paradise,
      We, newly Landing,
      Got thus Standing,
All Merry Boys, and Loyal,
    Our Pockets full of Pay,
    This Triumphal Day,
To make of our Skill a Tryal,
    Of our little little Skill :
    Let none then take it ill,
We must have no Denyal.

III.

We, who so often bang'd the Turk,
  Our Broad-sides speaking Thunder,
Made Belgium strike, and proud Dunkirk,
  Who liv'd by Prize, and Plunder,
And routed the Sebastian Shirk;
  We paid their Poops, and painted Beaks,
  Cleans'd before and aft their Decks,

Till

Till their Scuppers ran with Gore,
Whilst in as fast salt Water breaks;
But we are Friends of this no more:
Through this Crowd,
In a Cloud,
We have found a happy Shore,
And, newly Landing,
Got this Standing;
All Merry Boys, and Loyal,
Our Pockets full of Pay,
This Triumphal Day,
To make of our Skill a Tryal,
Of our little little Skill:
Let none then take it ill,
We must have no Denyal.

Besides the three before-named, who sang the precedent Song, there were in like manner habited, like Sea-men, six other Persons, who made a Winde-Musick.

The Musick in the Stage consisted of three Drums, and six Trumpets.

On the *East*-side, Winde-Musick, consisting of six Persons.

On two Balconies, within the *Arch*, Winde-Musick, consisting of twelve Persons.

On the *West*-Gallery were placed six Trumpets.

These, and all the other Musick, belonging to this Triumph, performed their Duty without Intermission, till such time, as His Majesty fronted the *Figure*, which represented *Thames*, and then ceased; upon which, *Thames* made the ensuing *Speech*,

Ten Moons, Great Sir, their Silver Crescents fill'd,
Since, mounted on a Billow, I beheld
You on the Bridg; but louder Joys there were,
That barr'd my Welcomes from Your Sacred Ear:

Now

Now I above my highest Bound have rear'd
My Head, to say what could not then be heard.

Hail, Mighty *Monarch!* whose Imperial Hand
Quiets the Ocean, and secures the Land;
This City, whom I serve with Neighb'ring Floods,
Exporting Yours, importing Foreign Goods,
With anxious Grief did long Your Absence mourn;
Now with full Joy she welcomes Your Return;
Your blest Return! by which she is restor'd
To all the Wealth remotest Lands afford.
At Your Approach I hasten'd to the *Downs*,
To see Your moving Forts, Your Floating Towns,
Your *Sovereigns*, big with Thunder, plow the Main,
And swimming Armies in their Womb contain.
You are our *Neptune*, every Port, and Bay
Your Chambers: the whole Sea is Your High-way.
Though sev'ral Nations boast their Strength on Land,
Yet You alone the Wat'ry World command.

Pardon, great *Sir*, fair *Cynthia* checks my stay;
But to Your Royal Palace, twice a day,
I will repair; there my proud Waves shall wait,
To bear our *Cæsar*, and His conqu'ring Fate.

We finde the Speech of the River *Tyber* on the like Solemnity, the Procession of the Senate, &c. attending on the two Brothers *Probinus*, and *Olybrius*, newly elected Consuls, in CLAUDIAN;

Est in Romuleo *procumbens Insula* Tybri,
Quà medius geminas interfluit alveus urbes
Discretas subeunte freto, pariterque minantes
Ardua turrigeræ surgunt in culmina ripæ.
Hìc stetit, & subitum prospexit ab aggere votum;
Unanimes fratres junctos, stipante Senatu,

Ire

Ire forum, ſtrictaſque procul radiare ſecures,
Atque uno bijuges tolli de limine faſces.
Obſtupuit viſu, ſuſpenſáque gaudia vocem
Oppreſſam tenuère diu, mox inchoat ore.
Reſpice, ſi tales jactas aluiſſe fluentis,
Eurota Spartane, *tuis. Quid protulit æquum*
Falſus olor, valido quamvis decernere cæſtu
Nôrint, & *ratibus ſævas arcere procellas ?*
En nova Ledæis *ſoboles fulgentior aſtris !*
Ecce mei cives ! quorum jam Signifer optat
Adventum, ſtellisque parat convexa futuris.
Iam per noctivagos dominetur Olybrius *axes*
Pro Polluce *rubens, pro* Caſtore *flamma* Probini.
Ipſi vela regent : ipſis donantibus auras,
Navita tranquillo moderabitur æquore pinum.
Nunc pateras libare Deis, nunc ſolvere multo
Nectare corda libet : niveos jam pandite cœtus
Naiades, & *totum violis prætexite fontem :*
Mella ferent ſylvæ : jam profluat ebrius amnis,
Mutatis in vina vadis : jam ſponte per agros
Sudent irriguæ ſpirantia balſama venæ.
Currat, qui ſociæ roget in convivia menſæ
Indigenas fluvios, Italis *quicunque ſuberrant*
Montibus, Alpinásque *bibunt de more pruinas :*
Vulturnúsque rapax , & Nar *vitiatus odoro*
Sulfure, tardatìsque ſuis erroribus Uſens :
Et Phaëthonteæ *perpeſſus damna ruinæ*
Eridanus, *flavæque terens querceta* Maricæ
Liris, &, Oebaliæ *qui temperat arva,* Galeſus.
Semper honoratus noſtris celebrabitur undis
Iſte dies ; ſemper dapibus recoletur opimis.
Sic ait, & Nymphæ, *patris præcepta ſequutæ,*

Q

Tecta

Tecta parant peplis ; oſtróque infecta coruſco,
Humida gemmiferis illuxit regia menſis.

An Iſle 'midſt *Tyber*, with her ſpreading ſides,
The City, and his Silver Waves divides :
Banks on each Hand, and Tow'r-crown'd Margents riſe,
Threatning with their approach the lofty Skies ;
Here ſtanding on a Summit, he ſurvai'd
The loving Brothers, and the Cavalcade ,
As on they march'd, bright Axes born before,
And double Rods brought from one ſingle Floor.
Amaz'd he ſtood, long e're his joy could make
Way for his ſtrugling Voice, at laſt he ſpake.
   Spartan Eurota, ſee, if thou could'ſt e're
Such Brothers boaſt : compar'd to theſe, what were
The Swan's fair Race, though well they knew the Ceſt,
And how to ſteer a Fleet with Storms diſtreſt,
New Stars, behold ! out-ſhine *Ledæan* Fires.
Behold my People, whom the Sky deſires:
For future Flames a place Heav'n ready makes.
Olybrius ſhall rule Night's duskie Ax
For *Pollux*, *Probine* ſhine for *Caſtor's* Star,
They Sails ſhall ſwell, and gently move the Air,
That Sailors through calm Seas may ſteer the Pine.
Now pay Libations, now drink freely Wine.
You, *Naiades*, draw forth your beautious Ranks,
And ſtrew with Violets your Fountain Banks:
Inebriated Streams, now overflow
Your Banks, turn'd Wine ; in Woods let Honey grow ;
The Meads ſweat healing Balm ; let one ſtrait all
The Neighb'ring Rivers to a Banquet call.

                                              All

All thofe, who wash th' *Aufonian* Mountain's Feet,
And drink cold *Alpine* Snow; *Vulturnus* fleet;
Strong-fented *Nar*; and *Ufens* Streams, that grow,
By wand'ring through their own *Meanders*, flow;
Eridanus too, who makes fuch pityous moan
For lofs of his lamented *Phaëthon*;
And *Liris* feaking off *Marica's* Groves;
Galefus, who *Oebalian* Fields improves.
This day our Waves fhall always keep in State,
This we with annual Feafts will celebrate.
This faid, the *Nymphs*, obeying, thither throng,
The Walls, and Roof, with ftately Arras hung:
His Wat'ry Court with Royal Purple fhone,
And Boards enchac'd with Pearl, and pretious Stone.

The River *Thames* having ended his *Speech*, the three Sea-men, who entertain'd the Nobility with the former Song, addreffed the following to His Majefty.

I.

King CHARLES, *King* CHARLES, *great* Neptune *of the Main!*
Thy Royal Navy rig,
And We'll not care a Fig
For France, *for* France, *the* Netherlands, *nor* Spain.
The Turk, *who looks fo big,*
We'll whip him like a Gig
About the Mediterrane;
His Gallies all funk, or ta'ne.
We'll feize on their Goods, and their Monies,
Thofe Algier *Sharks,*
That Plunder Ships, and Barks,
Algier, Sally, *and* Tunis,

Q 2 *We'll*

We'll give them such Tosts
To the Barbary Coasts,
Shall drive them to Harbour, like Conies.
Tan tara ran tan tan
Tan tara ran tan tara,
Not all the World we fear-a;
The great Fish-Pond
Shall be thine-a
Both here, and beyond,
From Strand to Strand,
And underneath the Line-a.

II.

A Sail, a Sail, I to the Offin see,
She seems a lusty Ship;
Hoise all your Sails a-trip:
We'll weather, weather her, whate're she be.
Your Helm then steady keep,
And thunder up the Deep,
A Man of War, no Merchant She;
We'll jet her on her Crupper;
Give Fire, Bounce, Bounce,
Pickeering Villains trounce,
Till Blood run in Streams at the Scupper.
Such a Break-fast them we shall,
Give with Powder, and Ball,
They shall need neither Dinner, nor Supper.
Tan tara ran tan tan
Tan tara ran tan tara,
Pickeering Rogues ne're spare-a;

With

With Bullets pink
Their Quarters;
  Until they ſtink,
  They ſink, they ſink,
Farewel the Devil's Martyrs.

III.

They yield, they yield; ſhall we the poor Rogues ſpare?
Their ill-gotten Goods,
Preſerv'd from the Floods,
That King CHARLES, *and we may ſhare?*
With Wine then chear our Bloods,
And, putting off our Hoods,
Drink to His MAJESTY *bare,*
The King of all Compaſſion:
On our Knees next fall
T' our Royal Admiral,
A Health for His Preſervation,
Dear JAMES *the Duke of* YORK,
Till our Heels grow light as Cork,
The ſecond Glory of our Nation.
  Tantara ran tan ton
  Tantara ran tan tara
  To the Royal Pair-a,
Let every man
Full of Wine-a
  Take off his Can,
  Though wan, though wan,
To make his Red Noſe ſhine-a.

    The

The Sea-men having ended their Song, the several forts of Musick performed their Duty, whilest His *Majesty* passed on towards *Cheap-side*.

At the *Stocks* the Entertainment was a Body of Military Musick, placed on a Balcony; consisting of six Trumpets, and three Drums: the Fountain there being after the *Thuscan* Order, venting Wine, and Water.

In like manner, on the Top of the great *Conduit*, at the Entrance of *Cheap-side*, was another Fountain, out of which issued both Wine, and Water, as in a Representation of *Temperance*; and on the several Towers of that Conduit were eight Figures, habited like *Nymphs*, with Escutcheons in one Hand, and Pendents, or Banners in the other: and between each of them Winde-Musick; the number, eight.

On the Standard also in *Cheap-side* there was a Band of Waits placed, consisting of six Persons.

THE

THE THIRD ARCH.

THE third Triumphal *Arch* stands near *Wood-street* end, not far from the place where the *Cross* sometimes stood.

"It represents an *Artificial Building of two Stories*, one "after the Corinthian way of *Architecture*, the other "after the Composite, *representing the* TEMPLE *of* CONCORD; "with this Inscription *on a Shield*,

ÆDEM

CONCORDIÆ

IN HONOREM OPTIMI PRINCIPIS,

CUJUS ADVENTU

BRITANNIA TERRA MARIQ. PACATA,

ET PRISCIS LEGIBUS REFORMATA EST,

AMPLIOREM SPLENDIDIOREMQ.

RESTITUIT

S. P. Q. L.

CONCORD was reputed by the *Romans* in the number of their Goddesses, as we finde in JUVENAL,

Cui colitur Pax, atque Fides, Concordia, Virtus;

and had several Temples, upon various occasions, vowed, and dedicated to her. There arose a dangerous Feud, which continued for some Years, between the Senate, and People of *Rome:* whereupon *Furius Camillus*[*], turning himself to the Capitol, desired of the Gods, that he might speak, and act that, which might tend to the benefit of the Commonwealth, and reconciliation of the two dissenting
Parties;

[*] *Anno U. C. CCCXXII.*

Parties; and to that end vowed a Temple to C o n c o r d. Wherefore having called the Senate, after a long, and various Debate, upon
certain Conditions, brought the Senate, and People to an Agreement.
Which Temple, according to his Vow, by a Decree of the Senate, was
erected, and dedicated to C o n c o r d. This is mention'd, though ob-
scurely, *in tabulis Capitolinis*; but plainly, by O v i d *:

Fastor.
Lib. I.

> *Nunc bene prospicies* Latiam C o n c o r d i a *turbam,*
>   *Nunc te sacratæ constituère manus.*
> Furius, *antiquus populi superator* Etrusci,
>   *Voverat, & voti solverat ille fidem.*
> Caussa, quòd à Patribus sumptis secesserat armis
>   Vulgus, & ipsa suas Roma timebat opes.

> Now maist thou C o n c o r d, *Rome* with kindness see,
> Now sacred Hands a Fane erect for thee.
> *Furius,* who conquer'd the *Etrurian,* made
> A solemn Vow, which solemnly he paid.
> Because the People did their Princes beard,
> Taking up Arms; and *Rome* her own Wealth fear'd.

† Anno U.C.
DXXXV.

    The like Vow was made by *L. Manlius* †, upon a Mutiny of the
Army under his Command, and the Year after the Temple was erected, and dedicated by *M.* and *C. Atilius Regulus,* elected for that pur-

Anno U.C.
DCXXXII.

pose. So in the Sedition of *Gracchus* *, who encamped on the *Aventine,*
and refused the Conditions offered him by *L. Opimius* Consul, the
Consul immediately vowed a Temple to C o n c o r d; and after his
Victory over those seditious Conspirators, dedicated it *in Foro.* Which
did highly incense the Communalty, who thought that C o n c o r d
could not be founded on the Slaughter of their Fellow-Citizens: and
some of them adventured to add this Inscription to the Title of the
Temple,

    VECORDIÆ. OPUS. ÆDEM. FACIT. CONCORDIÆ.

                                      We

We finde mention of the like Temples in several Inscriptions, collected by *Gruter*; as in this,

D.N.Constantino.Maximo.Pio.Felici.Ac.
TRIUMPHATORI. SEMPER AUGUSTO. OB. AMPLI
CATAM.TOTO.ORBE.REM.PUBLICAM.FACTIS.CON
SILIISQ.

S.   P.   Q.   R.

DEDICANTE. ANICIO.PAULINO.JUNIORE. C.V. COS
ORD. PRÆT. URBI

S.   P.   Q.   R.

ÆDEM. CONCORDIÆ. VETUSTATE. COL-
LAPSAM. IN MELIOREM. FACIEM. OPERE
ET. CULTU. SPLENDIDIORE. RESTITUE
RUNT.

And in another not unlike the former,

ÆDEM. CONCORDIÆ. VETUSTATE. COLLAPSAM
AMPLIOREM.OPERE.CULTUQ.SPLENDIDIOREM
RESTITUIT.

S.   P.   Q.   R.

"In the Spandrils of the Arch there are two Figures, in Female Habits,
"leaning: One representing PEACE, the other TRUTH. That of Peace
"hath her Shield charged with an Helmet, and Bees issuing forth, and
"going into it; the Word,

PAX BELLO POTIOR.

"TRUTH, on the other side, in a thin Habit, on her Shield TIME,
"bringing Truth out of a Cave; the Word,

TANDEM EMERSIT.

R   "Over

" *Over the great Painting upon the* Arch *of the* Cupula *is reprefented*
" *a large* Geryon *with three Heads crowned ; in his three right-Hands,*
" *a* Lance, *a* Sword, *and a* Scepter ; *in his three left-Hands the three*
" *Efcutcheons of* England, Scotland, *and* Ireland : *before him the King's*
" *Arms with three Imperial Crowns ; beneath, in great Letters,*

CONCORDIA INSUPERABILIS.

Geryon, Son of *Chryfaor,* and *Caliirrhoe ,* according to *Hefiod,*
was feigned by the *Poëts* to have three Heads, and as many Bodies, who
was fubdued by *Hercules.* Of whom Virgil [*],

*   ———nam maximus ultor*
Tergemini nece Geryonis *fpoliisque fuperbus,*
Alcides aderat, taurósque bác victor agebat
Ingentes, val'émque boves amnémque tenebant.

Here the Revenger great *Alcides* ftood,
Proud with the triple *Geryon's* Spoils, and Blood ;
The Conqu'rour drave his Cattel to thefe Grounds,
Whofe Head poffefs'd the Vale, and River's Bounds.

And more largely Silius Italicus [†],

Qualis Atlantiaco *memoratur littore quondam*
Monftrum Geryones *immane tricorporis iræ :*
Cui tres in pugna dextræ varia arma gerebant ;
Una ignes fævos, aft altera ponè fagittas
Fundebat, validam torquebat tertia cornum,
Atque uno diverfa dabat tria vulnera nifu.

——— So (famous in a former Age)
That horrid Monfter of a Triple rage,
Geryon, fought on the *Atlantick* Shore :
Whofe three Right-Hands three fev'ral Weapons bore ;
One cruel Flames, behind him th'other drew
His Bow, the third his trufty Jav'lin threw ;
And dealt three fev'ral ways, at once, a Wound.

             The

The Origination of this Fable, and its Significations, are variously related. *Palæphatus* supposed him to have been feigned by the *Poets* to have three Heads, because he had his Birth in a City on the *Euxine* Sea, called *Tricarenia*, that is, of *three Heads*. Others, that it related to the three Brothers, who unanimously govern'd *Spain*. And indeed, that *Spain*, by reason of its Tripartite Division, was signified by the *Hieroglyphick* of *Geryon*, is not onely the Opinion of some Authours, but appears from a Coyn of the Emperour *Hadrian*, the third time *Consul*, in which there is a three-headed Image leaning on a Spear; either to signifie his Peragration of *Spain*, or his Origination from thence. Others have referr'd this to the Vices of Speech, Body, and Soul, which *Hercules* overcame; which is confirm'd from the three Apples ordinarily held in one Hand of *Hercules*, still to be seen in a Statue of his in the *Farnese's* Palace at *Rome*, which, *Suidas* says, alluded to the same.

" *On the top of the* Cupula CONCORD, *a Woman in her* " *right-Hand holding her Mantle; in her left-Hand a Caduceus; un-* " *der her Feet a Serpent strugling, which she seems to tread down.*

That a Serpent was a *Hieroglyphick* of Enmity, and War, (for which cause it is presented trampled under the Feet of CONCORD) appears from many Writers, Histories, and Medaigles. ARTEMIDORUS *, A Serpent signifies a Disease, and brings Enmity: according as that hurts any one in his Dream, so shall his Disease, and Enemy.* And ACHMET, *Serpents generally, according to their proportion, signifie Enemies.* NICEPHORUS, Patriarch of *Constantinople*,

Killing a Serpent, think your Enemy you kill.

So DIODORUS says, that, according to the *Ægyptians, A Serpent is the Symbol of Hatred.* VIRGIL, describing *Alecto*, endeavouring to raise a War betwixt *Turnus* and *Æneas*, feigns her with two Snakes erect upon her Head;

——————— *Flammea torquens*
Lumina, cunctantem, & quærentem dicere plura
Reppulit, & GEMINOS erexit crinibus ANGUES:
Verberáque insonuit, validóque hæc edidit ore.

R 2   Rowling

Rowling her bloody Eyes, she drives him back,
Labouring Requests, and once again to speak:
Then with two Serpents from her Snaky Hair
She scourging him did thus her Rage declare.

ÆSCHYLUS, of a Dream of *Clytemnestra,*

Τεκεῖν δράκοντ᾽ ἔδοξεν, ὡς αὐτὴ λέγει,
ἐν σπαργάνοισι παιδὸς ὁρμίσαι δίκην.
Τῆς θεσφάτης χρὴς τῆν πεγκῆς ἔδωκε,
Ἀντὴ προσέσχε μαζὸν ἦ τ᾽ ἐνέφρε.
Ὡς ἐν γάλακτι θρόμβος ἐμιάχθη σκότον.

As she reported, in her Dream she thought,
Forth to the World that she a Serpent brought,
Swath'd like a tender Infant wanting meat,
And, pitying, lays the Monster to her Teat.
Milk issued forth commix'd with clotted gore.

From whence *Orestes* immediately conjectured she was to die by his
Hand.

Δεῖ τοί νιν, ὡς ἔθρεψεν ἔκπαγλον τέρας,
Θανεῖν βιαίως· ἐκδρακοντωθεὶς δ᾽ ἐγὼ
Κτείνω νιν, ὡς τούνειρον ἐννέπει τόδε.

So she, who gave the Monster life, and breath,
Should therefore suffer by a violent Death:
And I, like an enraged Serpent, should
Kill her my self, and her sad Dream unfold.

Plut. in Gracch. Which may further be illustrated from several events, TIBERIUS
GRACCHUS, *in his Bed, was clasp'd about by two Serpents. Which Prodigie when the South-sayers had considered, they counselled, that he should neither kill both, nor let both escape: and further said, that if he kill'd the Male, it
would cost his own life; if the Female, his Wife* Cornelia's. TIBERIUS, *bearing affection to his Wife, and withall thinking it more agreeable, that he, being
the elder, should die first, kill'd the Male, and let the Female escape: and
                                                                    not*

not long after died. The same evil consequence we finde in the History of C. HOSTILIUS MANCINUS[†]; *who, as soon as he had gone aboard a Ship, in order to his Voyage to* Numantia, *on a suddain heard a Voice cry,* Stay, MANCINUS. *Whereupon he return'd back, and, at* Genoa, *going aboard again, found a Serpent in the Ship, which escaped from him. He was overthrown, and delivered up to his Enemies.* And VALERIUS MAXIMUS [*] says, that in the dissension of *M.* Fulvius Flaccus *about making some* Laws, *two black Serpents, sliding into the* Cell *of* Minerva, *portended intestine Murders.* Thus we finde them generally to portend sad Events, but particularly they were the *Hieroglyphick* of *War,* and *Devastation.* This appears from that known Story of *Homer,* where he tells us, that while the *Grecians* were sacrificing at *Aulis,* they saw a Dragon devour eight young Sparrows, with the Damm, and makes the Prophet *Calchas* [†] interpret it the duration of the War for nine years.

[† Obsequens De Prodigiis cap. lxxxiii.]

[* Lib. i. cap. li. vol.]

[† Iliad. C.]

Ὡς ὅ[..] κατὰ τλα' ἕφαγε στρωθοῖο, ὦ κυ[..];
Ὀκλὼ, ἀτὰρ μλίω ὀκλω ἦν, ἣ τέκα τέκνα·
Ὡς ἡμεῖς τοσσαῦτ' ἔτεα πτολεμίζομεν αὐθι,
Τῷ δεκάτῳ δὲ πόλιν αἱρήσομεν εὐρυάγυιαν.

For, as this Serpent, which from th' Altar sprung,
Devour'd the woful Mother, and her Young,
Which with her tender Issue make up nine:
So many Years the Destinies design
This War shall last, and we the Tenth destroy
The lofty Bulwarks of well-builded *Troy.*

Where the Dragon signified the War; the number of the Birds, the Continuation of it. So when *Hannibal,* in a Dream, saw a Serpent of vast magnitude throwing down Rocks, Woods, and Towns, and enquired of the Gods the meaning of it, they return'd this Answer[†]

[† Silius Ital. lib. iii.]

BELLA *vides optata tibi;* te maxima BELLA,
Te strages nemorum, te toto turbida cœlo
Tempestas, cædésque virûm, magnæque ruinæ
Idæi generis, lachrymosáque fata sequuntur.
Quantus per campos populatis montibus actas
Contorquet sylvas squallenti tergore SERPENS,

Et

Et latè humectat terras spumante veneno :
Tantas,perdomitis decurrens Alpibus, atro
Involves BELLO Italiam : *tantóque fragore*
Eruta convulsis prosternes oppida muris.

————————Thou do'st see
The War so much desir'd, and sought by Thee.
Thee greatest Wars attend ; the dreadful Fall
Of Woods, and Forests, with high Storms, that all
The Face of Heav'n disturb ; the Slaughter Thee,
And Death of Men ; the great Calamity
Of the *Idæan* Race, and saddest Fate
Do follow, and upon thee daily wait.
As great, and terrible, as that dire Snake,
Which now the Mountains with his Scaly Back
Depopulates, and drives the Forests through
The Fields before him, and doth Earth imbrue
With frothy Poison : Such thou, having past,
And overcome the *Alps*, with War shalt wast
All *Italy* ; and, with a Noise as great,
The Cities, and their Walls, shalt ruinate.

Mr. Ross.

Which is evidently seen in some Medaigles of the *Roman* Emperours,
as in this Reverse of *Augustus's*.

Volus. Cæs.
Aug.pag. xli.

Where two Serpents, that is, the Hostility, and Dissension of the *Roman*
Empire, divided into two Factions, that of *Augustus*, and *Antony*, are se-
parated

parated by an intervening Victory; that of *Augustus* at *Actium*, and
Alexandria. That upon these Victories this Coyn was stamp'd, may
be collected from the Inscription on the other side, C Æ S A R I M P. VII.
that is *annus* u. c. ᴅᴄᴄxxɪᴠ. in which * Year he triumph'd for the　*Dio, Lib II.*
two Victories before-mention'd, The same is to be seen in a Reverse
of *M. Antony's.*

　　　　　　　　　　　　　　　　　　　　　　　　　Goltz. Ỳul.
　　　　　　　　　　　　　　　　　　　　　　　　　Cæf. pag.
　　　　　　　　　　　　　　　　　　　　　　　　　xlviii.

Where a Woman (supposed to be *CONCORD*, with the Face
of *Octavia*, Sister to *Augustus*, and Wife to *M. Antony*,) in a long Stole,
holding in her left Hand a pure Spear, in her right a Pontifical Vessel,
parts two Serpents, signifying the Armies of *Augustus*, and *Antony.* Which
Interpretation of this Coyn is very much confirm'd from History. For
this Pacification, obtain'd by the Prudence of *Octavia*, happened *anno*
u. c. ᴅᴄᴄxᴠɪ. *Agrippa*, and *Gallus*, being *Consuls.* That this Coyn
was stamp'd after the Year ᴅᴄᴄxɪᴠ. (the time of the Peace between　*Vide Pighi*
Sext. Pompey, *C. Cæf. Octavianus*, and *Antony*,) appears from the In-　*Annal. ad*
　　　　　　　　　　　　　　　　　　　　　　　　　　　　　　　　rum annorum.
scription on the other side, M. ANTONIUS IMP. COS. DESIG.
ITER. ET. TERT. for *Appian* * says, that, after that Peace, the　* *De Civil.*
Consulships were appointed for the next four Years. For the first, *An-* *Bel. Lib. v.*
tony, and *Libo*(which *Antony* had been *Consul* before with *Julius Cæsar*;)
next, *Cæsar*, and *Pompey*; after them *Ahenobarbus*, and *Sossius*; last,
Cæsar, and *Antony*: τ⌒τα ᾖ τίν μίσσίω ᾖμίδον, then to become the third
time Consuls.

　　" On the West-side, the third great Figure, a Woman standing at the
　" Helm of a Ship; in her left Hand, a Cornu-copiæ; the Word,

FORTUNÆ REDUCI.

FORTUNE was not more various, and unconstant in her
Motions, then those, that painted her, in their Descriptions. The first
　　　　　　　　　　　　　　　　　　　　　　　　　　　was

was *Bupalus*, who put a Celeſtial Orb (which *Pierius* unhappily chang'd, by the miſtake of one Vowel, into a Foal) on her Head, and a *Cornu-copiæ* in her left Hand; as we finde her in a Reverſe of a Coyn of the Emperour *Gallienus*, with this Inſcription, ΕΦΕΓΙΩΝ ΤΥΧΗ Afterwards, ſome ſeigned her either ſtanding upon a Stone, or the top of ſome Mountain expoſed to the Winds, or upon a Wheel : others, upon the Prow of a Ship, holding a Sail with both her Hands; which is frequent in *Greek* Medaigles. P A U S A N I A S makes mention of a Temple of *Fortune*, in which there was her Statue, holding a young *Plutus*, the God of Riches, in her Hand: as we finde her in A R I S T O P H A N E S*, to ſignifie, that ſhe was the Mother, and Nurſe of Wealth.   Some attributed Wings to her, as E U S E B I U S mentions.   H O R A C E‡,

*In Plut.

‡ Lib. iii. Od. 29.

> ——— ſi celeres quatit
> *Pennas, reſiguo quæ dedit.* ———

If ſhe her nimble Pinions wave,
I ſtraight reſign whate're ſhe gave.

The *Scythians*, both Wings, and Hands, but no Feet.   When A P E L L E S was asked, why he made *Fortune* ſitting, he anſwered, *Becauſe ſhe never ſtood.*   But we ſhall onely take notice of what is here before us.   In the ſame manner we finde her deſcribed in a Stone, inſculp'd on both ſides, with this *Inſcription* on one,

NUM. DOM. AUG. SACRUM. FORTUNÆ CONSERVATRICI HORRE
OR. GALBANORUM. M. LORINUS FORTUNATUS MAGISTER S. P. B. D.

with the Image of *Fortune*, holding in her left Hand a *Cornu-copiæ*, in her right the Helm of a Ship : and ſo we finde her too in a *Reverſe* of a Coyn of T R A J A N the *Emperour*, mention'd by O c c o.   The like ſays L A C T A N T I U S*, *Effingebatur quidem Fortuna cum Cornu-copia, & Gubernaculo; tanquam opes tribuere putaretur, & humanarum rerum regimen obtinere :* Fortune *was made with a Cornu-copia, and the Helm of a Ship, as if ſhe were reputed the Diſpoſer of Wealth, and had the Government of Humane Affairs.* And P L U T A R C H‡, after various inſtances on each ſide, at length concludes, that the *Roman* Empire ought more to *Fortune*, then to *Valour*, or *Prudence* : and therefore ſays, that, having left the *Perſians*, and *Aſſyrians*, ſhe lightly flew over

*Lib. iii.

‡ De fortuna Romano-rum.

Ma-

Macedonia, and preſently ſhe ſhaked off ALEXANDER; then paſ-
ſing through *Ægypt*, and *Syria*, often tryed the *Carthaginians* : but when
ſhe had once paſſed the *Tyber*, and entered the Palace, ſhe laid aſide her
Wings, put off her *Talaria*, and forſook her unfaithful, and ever-mu-
table Sphere, as if ſhe intended to ſtay there for ever.   Indeed the *Romans* did confeſs as much; who, having dedicated ſundry *Temples* to
Fortune, with all variety of Honour, in the moſt eminent places of the
City, never erected one to *Virtue*, or *Valour*, till the time of *Marcellus*,
that took *Syracuſe*; or of *Scipio Numantinus*, about the five hundred   † *Helvicus
ſixty and third year after the building of the City.   To *Prudence*   Chronolog.*
never dedicated to any.   Among the reſt of *Fortune's* Titles none   *75. d.*
more frequent, then this of REDUX, to whom we read that
DOMITIAN the *Emperour* built a *Temple*, mention'd by MARTIAL*,   *Lib. vii.

> *Hic ubi* FORTUNÆ REDUCI *fulgentia latè*
> *Templa nitent.* ————

> Here, where bright Fanes to RETURN'D FORTUNE ſhine.

Temples of the like nature are mention'd too by CLAUDIAN,

> *Aurea* FORTUNÆ REDUCI *ſi Templa priores*
> *Ob reditum vovère Ducum, non dignius unquam*
> *Hæc Dea pro meritis amplas ſibi poſceret ædes,* &c.

> If they to FORTUNE REDUX vow'd of old,
> Their Chiefs return'd with Conqueſt, Fanes of Gold;
> The Goddeſs never more deſerv'd then now,
> That we ſhould ſtately *Temples* her allow.

There are alſo many *Medaigles*, and thoſe antient, of ſeveral *Emperours* with the ſame *Inſcription*,

" *Above there are eight living Figures with Pennons, and Shields, repre-*
" *senting the four Cardinal* Virtues, *each with an Attendant.*
" Prudence, *on her Shield* Bellerophon *on a* Pegasus, *running his*
" *Javelin into the Mouth of a* Chimera ; the Word,

CONSILIO ET VIRTUTE.

Bellerophon was the Son of *Glaucus* King of *Corinth,* renown'd both
for Prudence, Courage, Beauty, and Modesty.   Of whom thus
HOMER[†],

Iliad. vi.

> Αὐτὰρ Γλαῦκ⊙ ἔτικτο ἀμύμονα Βελλεροφόντην·
> τῷ δὲ θεοὶ κάλλ⊙ τι, ἠ ἠνορέην ἐρατινὴ
> Ὤπασαν.————

————————— Glaucus Bellerophon,
In whom all Good concenter'd as in one :
And Heav'n this Prince a Pers'nage did afford,
Which all admir'd. ————

The *Poëts* feign many Stories of him.   They say, he went to *Prætus,*
King of the *Argivi,* by whom at first he was kindly entertain'd.   But being afterwards falsly accused by *Antea,* the Wife of *Prætus,* for offering
to tempt her Chastity,   he sent him to *Iobates,* King of *Lycia,* with a
Letter written purposely to have him kill'd. *Iobates,* to pleasure *Prætus,*
sent *Bellerophon* against the *Chimæra.*   But *Minerva,* the *Goddess* of
Prudence, and *Valour,* protected his Innocence.   Wherefore she bri-
dled *Pegasus,* and delivered it to him. Upon whom being mounted, he
slew the *Chimæra* with his Javelin.   After which Victory he sent him
against the *Solymi* (a Nation betwixt *Lycia,* and *Pamphylia*) and the
Amazons.   From whence he returned also Conquerour ; *Iobates,* mo-
ved with his Prudence, and Valour, gave him to Wife his Daughter
Philonöe, and afterwards dying,   left him Successour in his Kingdom.
Of which largely HOMER[*],

Ibd.

> Πρῶτα μὲν ῥα Χίμαιραν ἀμαιμακέτην ἐκέλευσε
> Πεφνέμεν· ἣ δ' ἄρ ἔην θεῖον γένος, οὐδ' ἀνθρώπων·
> Πρόσθε λέων, ὄπιθεν δὲ Δράκων, μέσση δὲ Χίμαιρα,
> Δεινὸν ἀποπνείουσα πυρὸς μένος αἰθομένοιο.

Kai

Καὶ τὸν μὲν καθέπεφνε, Θεῶν τεράεσσι πιθήσας.
Δεύτερον αὖ Σολύμοισι μαχήσατο κυδαλίμοισιν·
Καρτίσην δὴ τήν γε μάχην φάτο δύμεναι ἀνδρῶν.
Τὸ τρίτον αὖ κατέπεφνεν Ἀμαζόνας ἀντιανείρας.
    Τῷ δ' ἂρ ἀνερχομένῳ πυκινὸν δόλον ἄλλον ὕφαινε·
Κρίνας ἐκ Λυκίης εὐρείης φῶτας ἀρίστες
Εἶσε λόχον· τοὶδ' ἔ'τι πάλιν οἶκον δὲ νέοντο.
Πάντας γὰρ κατέπεφνεν ἀμύμων Βελλεροφόντης.
    Ἀλλ' ὅτε δὴ γίνωσκε Θεῶ γόνον ἠὺν ἐόντα,
Αὐτοῦ μιν κατέρυκε, δίδου δ' ὃ γε θυγατέρα ἥν·
Δῶκε δέ οἱ τιμῆς βασιληΐδος ἥμισυ πάσης.

First he commands him stern *Chimæra* kill :
This hideous Monster, of no Mortal Race,
A Dragon's Tail had, and a Lion's Face,
Back'd like a shaggy Goat, still belching Flame :
This by Divine Asistance he o're-came.
Next he against renowned *Solym* fought ;
This Victory, he said, was dearly bought.
He last against the *Amazons* prevail'd.
    But, when he saw all open Forces fail'd,
He fell to close contrivance, and did lay
An Ambuscade to kill him in his way ;
Not one return'd of all, that were employ'd,
All were by bold *Bellerophon* destroy'd :
But when he knew he was of Heav'nly Blood,
His onely Daughter he on him bestow'd,
Investing straight with half his Regal Power.

The *Chimæra* is in the same manner described also by HESIOD*,

* In Theogonia, vers. 319.

Ἡ δὲ Χίμαιραν ἔτικτε, πνέουσαν ἀμαιμάκετον πῦρ,
Δεινήν τε, μεγάλην τε, ποδώκεά τε, κρατερήν τε.
Τῆς δ' ἦν τρεῖς κεφαλαί· μία μὲν χαροποῖο λέοντΘ·
Ἡ δὲ Χιμαίρης· ἡ δ' ὄφιΘ· κρατεροῖο δράκοντΘ·

S 2   Πρῶτο

Πρόσθε Λέων, ὄπιθεν δὲ Δράκων, μέσση δὲ Χίμαιρα,
Δεινὸν ἀποπνείουσα πυρὸς μένος αἰθομένοιο.
Τὴν μὲν Πήγασός τε ἕλε, ἡ ἐσθλὸς Βελλεροφόντης·

She bore Chimæra *belching dreadful Fire,*
Mighty, and strong, extremely swift, and dire.
Three Heads the Monster had ; a Lion's *first,*
And next a Goat's, *a* Serpent's *last, and worst.*
A Dragon's Tail *she had, and* Lion's Face,
Back'd like a Goat, *belching out Flames apace ;*
Whom Pegasus *took, and stout* Bellerophon.

* Æneid.
VII.
VIRGIL * also makes a *Chimæra* on the Helmet of *Turnus*, vomiting
forth Fire ;

    Cui, triplici crinita jubâ, galea alta Chimæram
    Sustinet, Ætnæos efflantem faucibus ignes.
    Tam magis illa fremens, & tristibus effera flammis,
    Quàm magis effuso crudescunt sanguine pugnæ.

On's Crest *Chimæra*, through a triple Tyre
Of bushy Horse-Mains, breath'd *Ætnæan* Fire.
Strangely it roars, and Flame more fiercely glows,
When in the Battel blood in Rivers flows.

From that part of the History, wherein *Minerva* is said to bridle *Pega-*
sus for *Bellerophon*, there was built a Temple, and Statue of *Minerva* called Χαλινῖτις *Frænatrix*; as PAUSANIAS † relates.

† In Corin-
thiacis.
    That *Bellerophon* was the Son of *Glaucus*, King of *Corinth*, appears
from a Medaigle of the *Corinthians* yet extant, on the Reverse of which
is *Bellerophon* mounted on *Pegasus*, slaying the *Chimæra* with his Javelin :
on the other side VENVS, with this Inscription ΚΟΡΙΝΘΙΩΝ,
because at *Corinth* VENVS had a most splendid Temple. There
is also a Coyn of C. *Cæsar*'s, in which *Bellerophon* kills the *Chimæra*,
with this Inscription COL. JUL. COR. that is, *Corinth* the
Colony of *Julius Cæsar*. Because C. *J. Cæsar* restored the City of *Co-*
rinth,

,inth, utterly deſtroyed before by *Mummius*, as we finde in D I O, and in P AU S A N I A S in the beginning of his *Corinthiaca*.

What the Antients did denote by this Triple Form of *Chimæra*, is doubtful.   N Y M P H O D O R U S the *Syracuſan* ſays, that *Chimæra* was a Mountain of *Lycia*, which perpetually vomited forth Fire, on the top of which lived Lions, in the middle (where were ſpatious pleaſant Medows) Goats, at the bottom Dragons.   Which Mountain when *Bellephoron* had rendred habitable, he was ſaid to have ſlain *Chimæra*.   But *Antigonus Caryſtiue* ſays,   it ſignified onely the People of three ſeveral Nations conquered by *Bellerophon*.

"J U S T I C E, *on her Shield a Woman holding a Sword in one Hand, a* "*Balance in the other*; the Word,

QUOD DEXTERA LIBRAT.

Though this Deſcription of J U S T I C E, with a *Balance* in one Hand,   hath been by late Writers accounted modern,   yet it appears from *Occo* to have been antient,   who thus found her repreſented in the Reverſe of a Coyn of *Trajan* the *Emperour*,   with a *Caduceus* in the other Hand : if he miſtook her not for *Moneta Aug*.   conſtantly ſo deſcribed; as may be ſeen in the Coyns of *Antoninus*, and other *Emperours*,

TEM-

"TEMPERANCE, *a Viol in her left Hand, a Bridle in her right*
"*the Word,*

FERRE LUPATA DOCET.

"FORTITUDE, *a Lyon having the Arms of* England, *in an*
"*Escutcheon; the Word,*

CUSTOS FIDISSIMUS.

"*The internal Part of this Triumph, or Temple, is Round, the upper*
"*part Dark, onely enlightened by Artificial Lights; the lower part divided*
"*into ten Parts by Pilasters with Pedestals.*

"*Within the Temple are twelve living Figures, three placed above the*
"*Rest.*

"*The First the Goddess of the* Temple *in rich Habit, with a Cadu-*
"*ceus in her Hand, and a Serpent at her Feet.   Behind the Goddess, a*
"*Man in a Purple Gown, like a Citizen of* London, *presenting the* KING
"*with an Oaken Garland. Over the* KING's *Head,*

PATER PATRIÆ.

"*Over the Citizen's,*

S. P. Q. L.

OB CIVES SERVATOS.

There were several sorts of *Crowns* in use among the *Romans*, according to the variety of the Deserts of those, who were rewarded with
them ; *Obsidionales, Murales, Castrenses, Navales, Rostratæ, Ci-*
vicæ.

The *Obsidionalis* was given to him, who had rais'd a Siege ; which was
made of the Grass, that grew in the place besieged :   and this was accounted more ; honourable then any of the rest.   The first among the
Romans, that was rewarded with this sort of Crown, was *Q. Cincinnatus*;
after him *P. Decius*, and *L. Sicinius Dentatus, Calpurnius Flamma*, and
others.

The *Mural* Crown was the reward of him, that first scal'd the Walls,
and entred the place assaulted ; mention'd by SILIUS ITALICUS *,

Fulvius ut finem spoliandis ædibus, ære
Belligero revocante, dedit ; sublimis ab alto

Suggestu

Suggeſtu (magnis autor non futilis auſis)
Lavino generate, inquit, quem Soſpita Juno
Dat nobis, Milo, *Gradivi cape victor honorem,*
Tempora Murali cinctus turrita coronâ.

But when, from Plunder of the Town, agen
The *Gen'ral,* by the Trumpet's ſound, his Men
Had call'd (a Noble Cheriſher of great
Attempts) to *Milo,* from his lofty Seat,
He thus began; *Lanuvian* Youth, whom we
From *Juno Soſpita* receive, from me
This Martial Honour for thy Victory
Accept, and 'bout thy Tower'd Temples try
This Mural Crown.————

                              Mr. ROSS.

And in another place†,   † Lib. xv.

————*phaleris hic pectora fulget,*
Hic torque aurato circumdat bellica colla ;
Ille nitet celſus Muralis honore coronæ.

        ————here ſhining ſtood
One with rich Trappings on his Breaſt, and there
Another on his Warlick Neck did wear
A Golden Chain : this with a Mural Crown
Was honour'd, ————

    The *Caſtrenſis* belong'd to him, that firſt entered the Tents of the Ene-
my : which, in the Infancy of the *Roman* Empire , was made of *Leaves.*
With ſuch an one *Romulus* rewarded *Hoſtius Hoſtilius,* Grand-Father to
Tullus Hoſtilius, King of *Rome* : afterwards of *Gold.* This, without queſtion, is the ſame with that, which otherwiſe is call'd *Vallaris.*
    The *Corona Navalis,* or *Roſtrata,* (for they ſeem not to be diffe-
rent, however *Lipſius* diſtinguiſheth them) was the reward of him, that
firſt boarded the Enemie's Ship, and took it : with this ſort of Crown
                                                        POMPEY

Pompey *the Great* honoured *M. Varro*; and Augustus *Agrippa.* The Form of it is still preserv'd in the Coyns of *Agrippa,*

Goltz. An- gust. xxix.

x Æn. viii. This is it, which Virgil ✱ mentions,

Tempora Navali fulgent roftrata coronà,

His Brows, deck'd with a Naval Garland, fhone.

But that, which gave us occafion to mention thefe, is the *Corona Civica,* given to him, that in fingle Combat had refcued a Citizen, and ✝ Lib.i. flain the Enemy on the place : and this was made of *Oak.* Lucan ✝,

——— *Emeritique gerens infignia doni Servati civis referentem præmia quercum.*

——— Crown'd with an Oaken Wreath, Rewards for fuch, a *Roman* fav'd from Death.

✱ Lib. iii. Stilic. Claudian ✱,

Mos erat in veterum caftris, ut tempora quercus Velaret, validis fufo qui viribus hofte Cafurum potuit morti fubducere civem.

'Twas th' ancient Guife in Camps, an Oaken Bough Should wreath his Temples,who had flain a Fo, And off a Citizen in danger brought.

And

And in another place [1],

[1] De laude Serenæ.

Hunc cingit Muralis *bonos, hunc* Civica *quercus*
Nexuit, hunc domitis ambit Roſtrata *carinis.*

This *Mural* Honour crowns, that *Civick* Boughs,
This wreaths his Head with conquer'd Gallies *Prows.*

Theſe were ordinarily prefix'd the Entrance of the *Emperour's* Palaces, as being *populi Servatores.*   OVID[*],

[*] Faſt. Lib.1.

Ante fores ſtabis, mediámque tuebere quercum,
Protegat & noſtras querna corona fores.

Thou ſhalt protect the middle Oak before
The Gates ; let Oaken Garlands ſave our Dore.

In another place,

En domus hæc, dixi, Jovis *eſt ; quod ut eſſe probarem,*
Augurium menti querna corona dabat.

Behold, ſaid I, this is *Jove's* Houſe ; I know
By th' Oaken Wreath, that needs it muſt be ſo.

Which ſeems to be derived from JULIUS CÆSAR: of whoſe
Statues thus APPIAN, ſpeaking of the Honours decreed to him ;
There were ſeveral Figures inſcribed on his Effigies : on ſome a Crown of
Oak, as dedicated to the Saviour of his Countrey.   And DIO of *Au-*
guſtus ; When he denied the Monarchy, and diſcourſed of dividing the Pro-
vinces, it was decreed, that Laurels ſhould be ſet up before his Palace, and a
Crown of Oak hung over them, to ſignifie, that he was conſtantly overthrowing
his Enemies, and ſaving his Fellow-Citizens.   The memory of which
Honour conferred on him is preſerved in ſeveral of his Coyns : in one
there is a Crown of Oak betwixt two Branches of Laurel.

T   In

In another the same Crown betwixt two *CAPRICORNS* (he was born under that Sign) with a Globe , and the Helm of a Ship.

* Nat. Hift.
lib. xvi.
cap. xii.
In one this *Inscription*, within the Crown of Oak, SALUS HUMANI GENERIS: to which PLINY*, without question , alluded in those words, *Dedit* AUGUSTUS *Roftratam coronam* AGRIPPÆ, *fed* CIVICAM à *genere humano recepit ipfe.*

There are several reasons propounded by PLUTARCH, and others after him, why this Crown should be made of this material; but none so probable as this, because the Oak was sacred to JUPITER and JUNO *Confervatoribus,* Σωτῆρσι, and Πελώχοι.

The Habit of VENUS 'tis something difficult in particular to deliver ; the antient *Artifts* having been more willing to form her naked, as appears from the Statues of her still remaining in *Rome,* and from this *Poëm* of *ANACREON* upon *VENVS* engraved on a Basin,

Ἄγε τίς τόρευσε πόντον ;
Ἄγε τίς μαινόσε τέχνη, &c.

What bold Hand the Sea engraves,

Whilst its undermined Waves

In

In a Dishe's narrow round
Art's more pow'rful Rage doth bound?
See by some Promethean *mind*
Cytherea *there design'd,*
Mother of the Deities,
Expos'd naked to our Eyes
In all parts, save those alone,
Modesty will not have shown,
Which for Cov'ring onely have
The thin Mantle of a Wave:
On the Surface of the Main,
Which a smiling Calm lays plain,
She, like frothy Sedges, swims,
And displays her Snowy Limbs, &c.

Mr, STANLEY.

Yet, because there is something of it particular to her, we shall give some account of it from *CLAUDIAN*, who thus describes her Dress, when she was going to the Wedding of *HONORIUS* the *Emperour*:

------ *natum gremio* Cytherea *removit :*
Et crines festina ligat, peplumque fluentem
Allevat, & blando spirantem numine ceston
Cingitur, impulsos pluviis quo mitigat amnes,
Quo mare, quo ventos, irataque fulmina solvit.

Venus the Boy lays from her Breast;
Binds up her Hair, and tucks her flowing Vest;
Girds on her *Cestus* breathing pow'rful love,
Which calms swoln Rivers by a Deluge drove,
The raging Seas, rough Winds, and thund'ring *Jove.*

T 2   What

¹Iliad. ω'. What this *Cestos* is, may best be known from Homer¹, who is the
first, that mention'd it:

> Ἦ, ἡ ἀπὸ στήθεσφι ἐλύσατο κεςὸν ἱμάντα,
> Ποικίλον· ἔνθα δέ οἱ θελκτήρια πάντα τέτυκτο·
> Ἔνθ᾽ ἔνι μὲν φιλότης, ἐν δ᾽ Ἵμερος, ἐν δ᾽ ὀαριστύς,
> Πάρφασις, ἥτ᾽ ἔκλεψε νόον πύκα περ φρονεόντων.

> This saying, off she takes her curious *Cest*,
> Where all Allurements were of Love exprest,
> Dalliance, Desire, Courtship, and Flatt'ries, which
> The wisest with their Sorceries bewitch.

The *Roses*, and *Dolphin*, in the Hands of Cupid, signifie his Dominion on Land, and Sea : of which there is extant an *Epigram* of
Palladas,

> Ουκὶ μάτην παλάμαις κατέχω ΔΕΛΦΙΝΑ, ὁ ΆΝΘΟΣ·
> Τῷ μὲν γὰρ Γαῖαν, τῇ δὲ Θάλασσαν ἔχει.

> The *Dolphin* he, nor *Roses* holds in vain :
> In this Hand Earth, in that he holds the Main.

Anacreon,

> Ῥόδον ὦ φέριστον ἄνθος,
> Ῥόδον ἔαρος μέλημα, &c.

> ¹ Roses, of all Flow'rs the King;
> Roses, the fresh Pride o'th' Spring,
> Joy of ev'ry Deity;
> *Love,* when with the *Graces* he
> For the Ball himself disposes,
> Crowns his Golden Hair with Roses.

Of the *Dolphin* largely OPPIAN,

> Δελφῖνες δ᾽ ἀγέλησιν ἁλὸς μέγα κυαινέθεσιν,
> Ἔξοχον ἠνορέην τε, ἢ ἀγλαΐην κομόωντες,

'Ῥαου‾

'ραῆ τ' ἀκωλίιυ· διὰ γὰρ, βλλῷ ὅσϻ θάλασσαϼ
'Ἰσῆανίας, φλογίω ᾽τι σίλας ᾽αιμενων ἐπωπϻϊς
'Οξύσαϻϙϼ, χαὶ αχ᾽ ώ᾽ ὑπαῖϟωσϣϊα χαριϟϻϧαϻϚ,
Καὶ πι᾽ ἱωϽ φαμϙϟϡι εἰλυμϑϼϙ ῶϙϻϙϼ ἰχϟϊη.

      'Οσοι γὰρ χύϟϙσϛ μεϡ᾽ ϊμοϟϙϛ ἄϟϟϟϙ
'Αιϟϙϊ, ὃ θρωσϛ μεϡ᾽ ἀϟϛϟιϡϙ Λέοϟϙϛ·
'Οσϙϛ δελϛιϙϟϙϝ ϊϼ ϊϟϙϙϛϡϛϟϙϼ Δεϟϙϟϙϊη·
Τϙσϙϼ ᾽ᾑ ΔΕΛΑΦΪΝΕΣ ϊϼ ιϟϟύσϙϼ ϊϟϙϙϻϙϛ, &c.

The _Dolphin_ rules the Scaly Flocks, endow'd
With Strength, and Swiftneſs; of his Beauty proud:
He, like a Lance diſcharg'd, through Billows flyes,
And dazling Flames darts from his glaring Eyes,
Finding out Fiſh, that frighted ſculk in Holes,
Or Caves, and bed themſelves in Sand like Moles.

    As Eagles monarch it 'mongſt fearful Birds;
As Lions Tyrants act 'mongſt ſubject Herds;
As much as cruel Serpents Worms excel:
So _Dolphins_ Princes in the Ocean dwell.
No Fiſh dares them approach, nor be ſo bold
His Eyes, and dreadful Viſage to behold.
Far from the **Tyrant**, fearing ſuddain Death,
Frighted they fly; fainting for want of Breath.
But when the _Dolphin_, hungry, hunts out Food,
The Silver Frie in Troops amazed ſcud,
Filling each way with fear: then Caves, and Holes,
Rocks, Bays, and Harbours fill with frighted Shoals.
From all parts driven he ſelects the beſt,
Chooſing from Thouſands out a plenteous Feaſt.

  " _Of the nine leſſer Figures; the firſt bears, on a Shield, the King of_
" _Bees flying alone; a Swarm following at ſome diſtance: the Word,_

  REGE INCOLUMI MENS OMNIBUS UNA.

                                  " _The_

" *The Second, on his Shield, a* Teſtudo *advancing againſt a Wall* ; *the*
" *Word,*

CONCORDIÆ CEDUNT.

" *The Third, a Shield charged with Hearts* ; *the Word,*

HIC MURUS AHENEUS ESTO.

" *The Fourth, like a* Spread-Eagle *with two Heads* , *one of an* Eagle,
" *the other of an* Eſtrich ; *in the Mouth of the* Eſtrich *an* Horſe-ſhoe, *in*
" *the Talon of the* Eagle *a Thunderbolt* ; *the Word,*

PRÆSIDIA MAJESTATIS.

" *The Fifth, a Bundle of* Javelins ; *the Word,*

UNITAS.

" *The Sixth,* *two Hands joyned athwart the Eſcutcheon* , *as from the*
" *Clouds, holding a* Caduceus *with a Crown* ; *the Word,*

FIDE ET CONSILIO.

" *The Seventh,* Arms *laid down,* Guns, Pikes, Enſigns, Swords ; *the*
" *Word,*

CONDUNTUR, NON CONTUNDUNTUR.

" *The Eighth, a* Caduceus, *with a Winged Hat above, and Wings be-*
" *neath, two* Cornu-copiæs *coming out at the middle, ſupported by a Gar-*
" *land* ; *the Word,*

VIRTUTI FORTUNA COMES.

" *The Ninth, a Bright* Star *ſtriking a gleam through the midſt of the*
" *Eſcutcheon* ; *the Word,*

MONSTRANT REGIBUS ASTRA VIAM.

With theſe Figures is intermingled a Band of twenty four Violins.
The Baſes, and Capitals within this *Triumph,* are as Braſs, and the
Pillars Steel.
    The Triumph thus adorned , and the ſeveral Muſick playing, all
paſſed through, till ſuch time as His Majeſty came to the middle of the
Temple,

Temple, at which time the three principal living Figures, *viz.* CONCORD, LOVE, and TRUTH, who till then had not been ſeen, were, by the drawing of a Curtain, diſcovered, and entertained His Majeſty with the following Song.

I.

Comes not here the King of Peace,
 Who, the Stars ſo long fore-told,
From all Woes ſhould us releaſe,
 Converting Iron-times to Gold?

II.

Behold, behold!
Our Prince confirm'd by Heav'nly Signs,
 Brings healing Balm,
Brings healing Balm, and Anodynes,
To cloſe our Wounds, and Pain aſſwage.

III.

He comes with conquering Bays, and Palm,
 Where ſwelling Billows us'd to rage,
Gliding on a ſilver Calm;
 Proud Intereſts now no more engage.

Chorus,

Let theſe arched Roofs reſound,
 Joyning Inſtruments, and Voice,
Fright pale Spirits under Ground;
 But let Heav'n and Earth rejoyce,

We

We our Happiness have found,
He, thus marching to be Crown'd,
Attended with this Glorious Train,
From civil Broils
Shall free these Isles,
Whilst He, and His Posterity shall reign.

I.

Who follow Trade, or study Arts,
Improving Pasture, or the Plow,
Or furrow Waves to Foreign Parts,
Use your whole Endeavours now.

II.

His Brow, His Brow
Bids your Hearts, as well as Hands,
Together joyn,
Together joyning bless these Lands;
Peace, and Concord, ne'er poor,
Will make with Wealth these Streets to shine,
Ships freight with Spice, and Golden Ore,
Your Fields with Honey, Milk, and Wine,
To supply our Neighbours Store.

The first Song ended, CONCORD addressed her self to His Majesty, in these words,

Welcome, great Sir, to CONCORD's Fane;
Which Your Return built up again;
You have her Fabrick rear'd so high,
That the proud Turrets kiss the Skie.
Tumult by You, and Civil War
In Janus Gates imprison'd are.

By

By You, the King of Truth, and Peace;
May all Diviſions ever ceaſe!
Your Sacred Brow the bluſhing Roſe,
And Virgin Lily twin'd encloſe!
The Caledonian Thiſtle-Down
Combine with theſe t'adorn Your Crown!
No Diſcord in th' Hibernian Harp!
Nought in our Duty flat, or ſharp!
But all conſpire, that You, as Beſt,
May 'bove all other Kings be Bleſt.

The Speech ended, His Majeſty, at His going off, was entertained
with the following Song,

With all our Wiſhes, Sir, go on,
    Our CHARLES, three Nations Glory;
That Worlds of Eyes may look upon,
    Behinde, Sir, and before Ye;
Go great Exemplar of our Britiſh Story,
        Paternal Crowns aſſume,
        That then Your Royal Name
        May, regiſtred by Fame,
        Smell like a ſweet Perfume:
Not writ in Marble, Braſs, or Gold,
        Nor ſparkling Gems,
        Such as ſhine in Diadems,
    But where all Nations may behold
        With brighter Characters enroll'd,
On th' Azure Vellum of conſigur'd Stars;
        Who fix'd, with gentle Smiles,
        Two fluctuating Iſles,
And built well-grounded Peace on Civil Wars.

V

On

On the little Conduit, at the lower End of *Cheap-side*, were placed four Figures, or *Nymphs*, each of them having an Escutcheon in the one Hand, and a Pendent in the other.

In a Balcony, erected at the Entrance of *Pater-noster-Row*, were placed His Majestie's Drums, and Fife; the number of Persons, eight.

Between that and *Ludgate* there were two other Balconies erected: in one was placed a Band of six Waits; in the other, six Drums.

On the Top of *Ludgate* six Trumpets.

At *Fleet*-Bridge, a Band of six Waits.

On *Fleet*-Conduit were six Figures, or *Nymphs*, clad in White, each with an Escutcheon in one Hand, and a Pendent in the other; as also a Band of six Waits. And on the *Lanthorn* of the Conduit was the Figure of *Temperance*, mixing Water and Wine.

THE

LIBERTATI AUG
EX TINCTO BELLI CIVILI
INCENDIO CIVIBVS DOMI TEMDI
ARAM CELSISS CONSTR

THE FOURTH ARCH.

IN *Fleet-street*, near *White-Friers*, stands the fourth Triumphal Arch, representing the *Garden* of PLENTY; it is of two Stories, one of the *Dorick* Order, the other of the *Ionick*. The Capitals have not their juſt Meaſure, but incline to the Modern *Architecture*.

" *Upon the great Shield over the* Arch, *in large Capitals, this Inſcri-*
" *ption,*

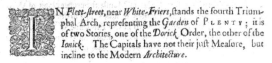

UBERITATI

A U G.

EXTINCTO BELLI CIVILIS INCENDIO,

CLUSOQVE JANI TEMPLO,

ARAM CELSISS.

CONSTRUXIT

S. P. Q. L.

To *Uberity,* or *Plenty,* there are frequent Dedications amongſt the
Reverſes

Reverses of the Coyns of the *Roman* Emperours; as of AUGUSTUS, and GALIENUS,

She is represented in a long Stole, or Mantle, the proper Habit of Women, holding in one Hand a *Patera*, or little Cup; in the other a *Cornucopia*. The latter is well known to be the Embleme of *Plenty*. Its original related by O v i d *: which, though unknown to few, the elegancy of the Relation will not give me leave to omit.

Metam. lib.ix. Fab. i.

> ———— *rigidum fera dextera cornu*
> *Dum tenet, infregit; truncáque à fronte revellit.*
> *Naiades hoc pomis, & odoro flore repletum*
> *Sacrarunt : divésque meo bona copia cornu est.*

> ———— my Brow he disadorns,
> By breaking one of my engaged Horns.
> The *Naiades* with Fruits, and Flow'rs this fill,
> Wherein abundant *Plenty* riots still.

The *Patera*, or little Cup, which she holdeth in the other Hand, is frequent in other Figures of Reverses; as

What

What is meant by EXTINCTO BELLI CIVILIS INCENDIO, *the extinction of the Flames of Civil War*, is fortunately known to us all, and may serve to explicate what follows, CLUSOQUE *FANI TEMPLO*, *the shutting of* Janus's *Temple* : a Rite instituted by NUMA, according to LIVY : *Numa Regno potitus Urbem novam, conditam vi & armis, Jure eam Legibusque ac Moribus de integro condere parat : quibus cùm inter bella assuescere videret non posse (quippe efferatis militiâ animis) mitigandum ferocem populum armorum desuetudine ratus,* Janum *ad infimum Argiletum, indicem Pacis Bellique fecit:* APERTUS, *ut in armis esse civitatem;* CLAUSUS, *pacatos circa omnes populos significaret.* NUMA, *being possess'd of the Kingdom, applyed himself to reform the new City, which was built by Force, and Arms, and to build it anew by Rites, Laws, and Institutions: with which perceiving, that in the midst of War it was not possible to be effected, by reason that their minds were made rough and fierce by Arms; he conceiving that the fierce People might by their disaccustomance be made mild, he built a Temple to* Janus *at the bottom of* Argiletus, *the signifier of Peace, and War: which being* OPENED, *shewed that the City was in Arms;* SHUT, *that they were in peace with all Nations.* This VARRO* confirms, *The* Janual *Gate is so call'd from* Janus *: and therefore an Image of* Janus *is plac'd there, and a Rite instituted by* NUMA POMPILIUS (*as* LUCIUS PISO *in his Annals relates*) *that it should be always* SHUT *but in the time of War. We finde no where, that it was* OPENED *in the time of* POMPILIUS. PLUTARCH, *in the* Life of NUMA, *There is at* Rome *a Temple also of* JANUS, *with a two-leav'd Gate, which they call* Polemopyle, *the Gate of War. For it was decreed, that in the time of War that Temple should be* OPEN ; *in Peace,* SHUT. *But* VIRGIL [†] *derives this Institution higher,*

* De ling. Lat. lib. iv.

† Æneid. vii.

> *Mos erat* Hesperio *in* Latio, *quèm protinus urbes*
> Albanæ *coluère sacrum, nunc maxima rerum*
> Roma *colit, cùm prima movent in prælia Martem;*
> *Sive* Getis *inferre manu lachrymabile Bellum,*
> Hyrcanisve Arabisve *parant, seu tendere ad* Indos
> *Aurorámque sequi,* Parthósque *reposcere signa.*
> *Sunt geminæ* BELLI PORTÆ (*sic nomine dicunt*)
> *Relligione sacræ, & sævi formidine* Martis.

Centum

Centum ærei claudunt vectes, æternáque ferri
Robora, nec custos absistit limine Janus.
Has (ubi certa sedet Patribus sententia pugnæ)
Ipse, Quirinali trabeâ, cinctúque Gabino
Insignis, RESERAT stridentia LIMINA Consul:
Ipse vocat pugnas, sequitur tùm cætera pubes,
Æreáque assensu conspirant cornua rauco.

There was an antient use in *Latium,*
Which *Alban* Towns held sacred, and now *Rome,*
Greatest in pow'r, observes; when they prepare
'Gainst *Arabs, Getes,* or fierce *Hyrcanians* War,
Or march to *India,* or the *Eastern* Main,
Or Ensigns from the *Parthians* to regain.
    Two Gates there be, are stil'd the PORTS OF WAR,
Sacred to *Mars* with reverential fear,
Shut with an hundred Iron, and Brazen Bands,
There in the Porch bifronted *Janus* stands.
Here, when the Senate have a War decreed,
The *Consul,* glorious in his Regal Weed,
And *Gabine* Robe, doth groaning Gates unbar,
In his own Person then proclaims the War.
The valiant Youth, attending, guard him round,
And doleful Trumpets *Diapasons* sound.

This Temple was shut several times, First in the Reign of NUMA POMPILIUS, as PLUTARCH* testifies. Next, after the second PUNICK *War,* by T. MANLIUS *Consul,* says LIVY†. Thrice by AUGUSTUS: once after the Victory at *Actium,* about the time of the Nativity of our SAVIOUR; and then most justly, when there was an *UNIVERSAL PEACE* over the whole World.

Of

Of which laſt there is a Monument extant at this day in *Spain* :

IMP. CÆS. DIVI F. AUGUSTUS PONT. MAX.
COS. XII. TRIBUNIC. POTEST. X. IMP. VIII.
ORBE MARI ET TERRA PACATO

TEMPLO JANI CLUSO

ET REP.P.R.OPTIMIS LEGIB.ET SANCTISS.INSTITUTIS REFORMATA
VIAM SUPERIORUM COSS. TEMPORE INCHOATAM
PRO DIGNITATE IMPERII LATIOREM LONGIOREMQUE
GADEIS USQUE PERDUXIT.

And at this time it may properly be ſaid to be ſhut at the fortunate arrival of our Sacred Sovereign into His Kingdoms, at what time there was a *GENERAL PEACE* throughout all *Chriſtendom.*

There is alſo a Coyn of AUGUSTUS, whoſe Reverſe is the Temple of JANUS ſhut; the *Inſcription*, JAN. CLU, not to mention that of NERO, PACE TERRA MARIQUE PARTA JANUM CLUSIT.

Guic. Au-
gust. Pag
lvii.
Augustin.
Dial. V.

" *Over the* Poſtern, *on the South-ſide of the Entrance is* BACCHUS, " *a Youth in a Chariot drawn by* Tigres ; *the Reins, Vine-Branches ; his* " *Mantle, a* Panther's *Skin; his Crown, of Grapes, and Ivy; a* Thyrſus "*in his left Hand, a Cup in his right : underneath,*

LIBER PATER.

" *The Painting over this repreſents* SILENUS *on his Aſs,* Satyres " *dancing round about, in Drunken and Antick Poſtures : the Proſpect, a* "*Vine-yard.*

The

* Saturnal.
lib. 1.cap.
xviii.

The Statues of Bacchus were of a very different form among the Antients. Macrobius *, *Liberi Patris simulacra partim puerili ætate, partim juvenili fingebantur; præterea barbata specie, senili quoque,* &c. *The Images of Bacchus were partly like Boys, others like Youths, some with Beards, some like Old men.* Ulpian[†], *Chorus's of all Ages contended in the Feasts of Bacchus, because they fram'd him of every Shape*; for they paint him a Boy, an Old, and a Young man. Of which Macrobius gives this Physical Reason, esteeming Bacchus to be the same with the Sun; *Because the Sun in the Winter Solstice may seem a Boy*, the days being then the shortest; but, by continual encreases in the Spring Æquinox, may seem a Youth; in the Summer Solstice, at his full age; afterwards in his diminution, an Old man. In the form of an Old man we finde him worship'd by the *Græcians*, under the Name of *Bassareus*, and *Bryseus*; and at *Naples* under the Name of *Hebon*: Macrobius in the same place. Of *Hebon* there is still remaining this Monument,

ΗΒΩΝΙ ΕΠΙΦΑΝΕΣΤΑΤΩΙ ΘΕΩΙ
ΙΟΥΝΙΟΣ ΑΚΥΛΑΣ ΝΕΩΤΕΡΟΣ
ΣΤΡΑΤΕΥΣΑΜΕΝΟΣ ΕΠΙΤΡΟΠΕΥΣΑΣ
ΔΗΜΑΡΧΗΣΑΣ.

So Pausanias * tells us of a Bearded Statue of *Bacchus* holding a Golden Cup in his Hand. But most frequently he is represented in the form of a Boy, or Youth. Tibullus[†],

Solis æterna est Phæbo Bacchóque juventus :
Nam decet intonsus crinis utrunque Deum.

Phæbus, and *Bacchus* must be ever young :
For uncut Hair to either God belong.

Ovid * of *Bacchus*,

——— *Tibi enim inconsumpta juventa,*
Tu puer æternus, tu formosissimus alto
Conspiceris cælo.———

——— still do'st thou enjoy
Unwasted Youth, eternally a Boy.

The

The *Poëts* feign him riding in a Chariot drawn either by Tigres, Leopards, or Lynces. STATIUS[†],   † Lib. iv.

> Liber *pampineos materna ad mœnia currus*
> *Promovet, effrenæ dextrà lævàque ſequuntur*
> *Lynces, & uda mero lambunt retinacula* tigres.

> Thence to his Mother's City *Bacchus* rides,
> Rein'd *Lynxes* by his Viny Chariot ſides,
> And *Tigres* lick'd the Harneſs moiſt with Wine.

HORACE,   * Lib. iii. Od. iv.

> *Hàc te merentem,* Bacche *pater, tuæ*
> *Vexère* tigres, *indocili jugum*
> *Collo trahentes.*————

> Bleſt *Bacchus* thee thy *Tigres* drew,
> Who Yoaks and Harneſs little knew.

OVID,   ¹ Metam. lib. iv. Fab. 3.

> ———— *tu bijugum pictis inſignia frænis*
> Colla premis lyncum. ————

> —————— thou hold'ſt in aw
> The ſpotted *Lynxes,* which thy Chariot draw.

These not onely drew his Chariot, but were his conſtant Companions ; as we finde in the Ship of *Bacchus,* (taken from the Mariners, whom he had turn'd into *Dolphins*) deſcribed by OVID[*],   * Metam. lib. iii.

> *Quem circa* tigres, *ſimulacráque inania* lyncum,
> *Pictarúmque jacent fera corpora* pantherarum.

> Stern *Tigres, Lynxes* (ſuch unto the eye)
> And ſpotted *Panthers* round about him lie.

X   His

His Ship is lively set forth by *Philostratus*[1]; which, or the like, is still to be seen in the Church of St. *Agnes* at *Rome*, formerly a Temple of *Bacchus*'s, in most exquisite *Mosaick* Work.

He was constantly crown'd either with Grapes, Ivy, or both. OVID*,

> *Ipse racemiferis frontem circumdatus uvis*
> *Pampineis agitat velatam frondibus hastam.*

> He, head-bound with a Wreath of clustred Vines,
> A Jav'lin shook, clasp'd with their leavy twines.

> *Non crines, non serta loco, dextrámque reliquit*
> *Thyrsus, & intactæ cecidérunt cornibus uvæ.*

> His Hair disorder'd now no Wreath adorns,
> His *Thyrsus* fell, plump Grapes drop from his Horns.

HORACE,

> —— *Deum*
> *Cingentem viridi tempora pampino.*

> —— a virdant Vine
> The God about his temples did entwine.

TIBULLUS,

> *Candide Liber ades, sic sit tibi mystica vitis,*
> *Sic hederâ semper tempora vincta feras.*

> *Bacchus* assist, so may the sacred Vine,
> So may fresh Ivy still thy Brows entwine.

So in *Achaia*, at the Feasts of *Bacchus* *, the Children having wash'd themselves in the River Meilichus, they put on Crowns of Ivy, and go to the Temple of Bacchus Æsymnetes.

                                                                    Hence

Hence *M. Antony* *, having aſſumed the Title of Νέος Διόνυσος *New* *Dio lib. xlviii.
Bacchus, cauſed the Coyns, ſtamp'd with his Image, to bear a Crown
of Ivy.

Gitz. 2nd Cæf. paq. xlvii.

And the Antients uſed this, as an Argument, to prove that *Bacchus* of
the *Grecians*, and *Romans*, was the ſame with *Oſiris* of the *Ægyptians*,
becauſe Ivy, which was ſacred to *Bacchus*, was in *Ægypt* called Χένοσις,
that is, *The Plant of* Oſiris.

Why *Bacchus*, and thoſe that drank, did wear a Crown of Ivy,
Athenæus gives this Reaſon amongſt the reſt, becauſe *there is great plenty
of it, and it grows of it ſelf, and is every where to be had, being not undelightful
for ſight, ſhading the Fore-head with its green Leaves, and Berries, and of a
body fit for binding, beſides that, cooling without any Carotique ſmell offenſive
to the Head.* The Wine-Bowls alſo were ordinarily adorn'd in the ſame
manner. VIRGIL,

-------------- *pocula ponam*
Fagina, cælatum divini opus Alcimedontis :
Lenta quibus torno facili ſuperaddita vitis
Diffuſos hederâ veſtit pallen'e corymbos.

-------------- two Beechen Cups I'll ſtake,
Which the divine *Alcimedon* did make :
Whereon with a ſmooth turn ſoft Vines he ſhapes,
And with pale Ivy cloaths the ſpreading Grapes.

ANACREON,

Ἡ χθὼν μέλαινα,
Ὅταν δύῃ, βέβρωται, &c.

X 2						Φιλατω

Πλοῦσιν ἀρπάλνι μας
Καὶ βότρυαι κατ' αὐΐ.

Vulcan come, thy Hammer take,
And of burnifh'd Silver make
(Not a glitt'ring Armour, for
What have we to do with War ?
But) a large deep Bowl, and on it
I would have thee carve no Planet,
Pleiades, Wains, nor Waggoners;
But to life exactly fhape
Clufters of the Juicy Grape ;
Whilft brisk *Love* their bleeding Heads
Hand in hand with *Bacchus* treads.

We finde him cloathed with the Skin of a *Tigre* (though that not
the onely one Garment he ufed) in *CLAUDIAN* :

—— *Lenisque fimul procedit* Iacchus,
Crinali florens hederà, quem Parthica *velat*
Tigris, & auratos in nodum colligit ungues.

——— So *Bacchus* march'd with Ivie crown'd,
Clad in a *Parthian* Tigre's fpotted Hide,
And Golden Claws in neat compofure ty'd.

A *Thyrfus* is a Spear adorn'd with Ivy at the upper end , which
Bacchus, and his Attendants, made ufe of to fuftain them in their drink.
Claudian , of *Bacchus*,

Ebria Mæoniis *fulcit veftigia* Thyrfis.

His *Lydian* Thyrfe fupports his reeling Limbs.

Paufanias , *The Statue* (of Jupiter) *is like unto* Bacchus; *for it hath*
Buskins inftead of Shoes, and it holds in one hand a Cup, in the other a Thyr-
fu. This *Thyrfus,* with a *Cornu-copiæ,* is the *Hieroglyphick* of Mirth
in

in a Coyn of *Faustina's* ; the Inscription *HILARITAS*. In one hand she holds a *Cornu copiæ*, in the other a *Thyrsus*, on a Spear, covered from one end to the other with Leaves, and Coronets.

Silenus, and the *Satyres*, were the constant deboist Companions of *Bacchus*. Of whom *Pausanias* * relates a Story told him by *Euphemus* a *Carian*, that, in a Voyage to *Italy*, by cross Winds, their Ship was forced beyond the *Streights* into the *Atlantick* Ocean, and was driven by the Tempest upon the Islands, called, by the Mariners, *The Islands of Satyres*. Whose Inhabitants were of a yellowish colour, and had Tails not inferiour to those of Horses. Who, as soon as they saw the Ship arrived, presently entered, and laid hold of the Women : so that the Mariners were forc'd, out of fear, to land them a Woman, whom the *Satyres* used not onely according to Nature, but abus'd all parts of her body: Nor were the young *Satyres* more devoted to *Venus*, then old *Silenus* to his Patron *Bacchus*. V I R G I L[1],

In Atticis

Eclog. VI.

——— Chromis *&* Mnasylus *in antro*
Silenum *pueri somno videre jacentem,*
Inflatum hesterno venas, ùt semper, Iaccho;
Serta procul tantùm capiti delapsa jacebant,
Et gravis attritâ pendebat cantharus ansâ.*

Say Muse, how *Chromis* and *Mnasylus* found
In's Cave *Silenus* sleeping on the ground,
O'th' last nights *Bacchus* swell'd (his usual guise)
Far from his Head his fall'n off Garland lies.

So O v i d*,

Metam. lib. iv. fab. ...

——— Bacchæ, Satyrique sequuntur,
Quique senex ferulâ titubantes ebrius artus
Sustinet, & pando non fortiter hæret asello.*

Light *Bacchides*, and skipping *Satyres* follow,
Whilst old *Silenus*, reeling still, doth hallow,
Who weakly hangs upon his tardy Ass.

Whence

Pausanias. Whence the *Eleans* *, in their Temple of *Silenus,* make *Drunkenness* delivering a Cup of Wine to him.

He was conceiv'd to be the Fosterer, and Educator of *Bacchus;* from
‖ Ecleg. iii. whence A U R E L I U S N E M E S I A N U S ‖ describes him with *Bacchus* in his Arms,

> *Cui Deus arridens horrendas pectore setas*
> *Vellicat, aut digitis aures adstringit acutas,*
> *Applauditve manu mutilum caput, aut breve mentum,*
> *Et simas tenero collidit pollice nares.*

> Smiling on him the God his bristly Hairs
> Plucks from his Breast, or nips his pricked Ears,
> His low Brow claps, and short'ned Chin, and grows
> Familiar, tweaking of his Saddle Nose.

* *Antiq. Rom.* And thus we finde *Silenus* in an antient Statue at *Rome* *. The *Satyres* were painted with Goats Horns, and Feet, to signifie the insatiableness
† *Mythol. lib. ii.* of their Lust. F U L G E N T I U S † ; *Satyri cum caprinis cornibus depin-guntur, quia nunquam novère saturari libidine; The Satyres are painted with*
* *Carm. lib. ii. Od. xix.* *Goats Horns, because their Lust is unsatiable.* H O R A C E * ,

> —— *aures*
> *Capripedum* Satyrorum *acutas.*

The Goat-foot *Satyres* pricked Ears.

" *On the North-side opposite,* C E R E S, *drawn in a Chariot by winged*
" *Dragons, and crown'd with Ears of Corn : in her left Hand, Poppy ; in*
" *her right, a blazing Torch. The Painting over her is a Description of*
" *Harvest; with*

CERES AUG.

That the Chariot of C E R E S was feigned to be drawn by *Dra-*
† *De raptu Proserp. lib. 4.* *gons,* appears from several places in the *Poëts.* C L A U D I A N ,

> ————*sinuosa* Draconum
> *Membra regens, volucri qui pervia nubila tractu*

> Signant,

Signant, & placidis humectant fræna venenis.
Frontem crista tegit, pingunt maculosa virentes
Terga notæ, rutilum squamis intermicat aurum.

——— she sinewy *Dragons* guides,
Who at high speed cut yielding Clouds in twain,
Their Snaffles frothing with delightful bane,
Crested their Fronts, Backs mark'd with freckling green,
Their Scales, when brissell'd up, Gold shines between.

And immediatly after,

——— *fulvis* SERPENTIBUS *attigit* Iden.

With yellow SERPENTS drawn she *Ida* reach'd.

OVID*,   * Fast. IV.

Dixit, & egrediens nubem trahit, inque DRACONES
Transit, & alifero tollitur axe Ceres.

Then going forth, a Cloud she draws, through Skies,
With *Dragons* drawn, her swift-wheel'd Chariot flies.

And a little before, of the same **Goddess**,

Quo simul ac venit frænatos curribus ANGUES
Junxit, & æquoreas sicca pererrat aquas.

Her harness'd Serpents in her Chariot puts,
And dry her way through swelling Billows cuts.

Where we see promiscuously used *angues*, and *dracones*. So the Rod
of *Mercury*, which is perpetually represented with Serpents about it,
by *Martial* is encompass'd by a *Dragon* :

Cyllenes cæl ique decus, facunde minister,
Aurea cui torto virga DRACONE nitet.

                                                        Heaven

Heaven and *Cyllenes* Joy; Speaker divine,
A Golden Dragon on thy Wand doth shine.

* De Bello Gallico. And Claudian * speaking of the Golden Fleece kept by a Dragon,

——— *insopitisque refusum*
Tractibus aurati custodem velleris Anguem.

The watchful *Dragon* kept the Golden Fleece.

The memory of *Ceres* her Chariot drawn by *Serpents* is preserv'd likewise in several old Marbles, and this *Medaigle*,

1 Georg. 1. The reason why *Poppy* should be attributed to *Ceres*, and from thence be call'd by Virgil *Cereale papaver*, is variously rendered by Servius: *Vel quod est esui sicut frumentum: vel quo Ceres usa est ad oblivionem doloris; nam, ob raptum Proserpinæ vigiliis fracta, gustato eo acta est in soporem: vel quia pani adspergatur.* Either because it is fit to eat, as Corn: or because Ceres used it to procure a forgetfulness of her grief; for, being wearied with continual watchings in pursuit of her Daughter Proserpina stoln from her, upon tasting of it, she fell asleep: or else because 'tis * Cornutus de Diis. sprinkled upon Bread. But the *Mythologists*, who esteem *Ceres* to be the same with the *Earth*, make it onely a Symbol of the Fecundity of it; or, from its orbicular Figure, to signifie the rotundity of the Earth; from its inequality, the Vallies, and Mountains; from the multiplicity of its Grains, the vast multitude of Men, and Animals. For which reason the fertile Countrey of *Sicily* was sacred to her, which she contended for with *Vulcan*; and, in token of the Victory, the *Sicilians* dedicated her Statue with a little Image of Victory on her Hand. Which Statue
Cicero

CICERO [1] makes mention of. These *Poppies* are mention'd by several of the *Poëts* ; as by

1 *Contra Verrem.*

CALLIMACHUS,

——————— γίλο δ χuεἰ
Στίμμαϊα, ᾗ μάκωνας. ——————

Poppies she took, and Garlands in her Hand.

THEOCRITUS,

——————— ἁ δὲ γελάσαϊα
Δερίγμαϊα, ᾗ μάκωνας ἐν ἀμφοτέρησιν ἔχοισα.

In either Hand the Corn, and Poppies had.

Porphyry, quoted by *Eusebius* *, says, that *Ceres* was crown'd with Ears of Corn, about which were several Branches of *Poppy*, which were the Symbols of *Fertility*.

* *De Præpar. lib. iii*

She was accounted by the Antients the Goddess, that first delivered to Mankind the Art of Tillage, whence they usually crown'd her with Ears of Corn. TIBULLUS,

> *Flava* Ceres, *tibi sit nostro de rure coroná*
> *Spicea*—————

O yellow *Ceres*, round thy Golden Locks,
Place Garlands taken from our Countrey Shocks.

OVID,

> *Flava* Ceres, *tenues spicis redimita capillos,*

Ceres, whose slender Hairs Corn-ears do bind.

Or put them in her Hand. So in the Reverse of a Coyn of *Julia Pia*,

Y   there

there is one leaning with her left Hand on a Spear, holding in her right
Hand an Ear of Wheat, with this Inscription, *CEREREM.*

She is frequently described with a Torch in her Hand, from that
known Story of her searching after her Daughter, stoln, and carried away
by *Pluto* out of *Sicily.* Of which Claudian*,

De raptu
Proserp.

Accingor lustrare diem, per devia rerum
Indefessa ferar: nullâ cessabitur horâ.
Non requies, non somnus erit, dum pignus ademptum
Inveniam, gremio quamvis mergatur Iberæ
Tethyos, & rubro jaceat vallata profundo.
Non Rheni glacies, non me Ripæa tenebunt
Frigora: non dubio Syrtis cunctabitur æstu, &c.
Sic fatur, notæque jugis illabitur Ætnæ,
Noctivago tedas inflammatura labori.

I'll search the day, no hour shall stop me hurl'd
Unwearied through all Cranies of the World;
No rest, no sleep, till my dear Pledge be found,
Though she lie hidden in th' *Iberian* Sound,
Or the Red-Sea. *Riphæan* Frosts, nor *Rhyne,*
Crusted with Ice, shall hinder my Design:
Nor yet the doubtful *Syrts* with wallowing Tides.
This said, to *Ætna's* Top she makes a flight,
Kindling her Torch for bus'ness of the Night.

So

So Pausanias* mentions a Statue of *Ceres*, holding in her right   * In *Asca-*
Hand a Torch, with her left Hand laid upon a Statue adjoyning, cal-   *dics.*
led *Despoina.* Statius†,   † *Thebaid.*
                                                                      lib. xii.

> *Qualis, ab Ætnæis accensâ lampade saxis,*
> *Orba* Ceres *magnæ variabat imagine flammæ*
> *Ausonium Siculúmque latus, vestigia nigri*
> *Raptoris, vastósque legens in pulvere sulcos.*

> Rob'd *Ceres* so at an *Ætnean* Stone
> Kindled her Torch, which blazing she drives on,
> Reprinting *Pluto's* steps on either Coast,
> Plowing up dusty Clouds in Furrows vast.

Ovid*,   * *Fastor.*
                                                                      lib. iv.

> *Illic accendit geminas pro lampade pinus :*
>   *Hinc* Cereris *sacris nunc quoque tæda datur.*

> There for a Torch two Pines the Goddess lights :
> Since, they with Tapers celebrate her Rites.

From whence she was call'd *Dea tedifera* :

> *Et per* tediferæ *mystica sacra* Deæ.

The like we meet with in the Collection of Gruter.

CERERI AUGUST.
MATRI. AGR.
L. BENNIUS. PRIMUS
MAG. PAGI.
BENNIA. PRIMIGENIA
MAGISTRA FECER.
GERMANICO. CÆSARE. II.
L. SEIO. TUBERONE. COSS.
DIES. SACRIFICI. XIII. K. MAI.

Y 2   " *On*

" *On the Weſt-ſide of the Arch, over the* South Poſtern, *the Goddeſs*
" Flora, *in a various-coloured Habit; in one Hand, Red and White*
" Roſes; *in the other*, Lilies: *on her head, a Garland of ſeveral Flowers.*
" *The Painting over this, a Garden with Walks, Statues, Fountains,*
" *Flowers, and Figures of Men and Women walking.*

The Story of this Goddeſs Flora is variouſly related : we ſhall
onely take notice of the account *Lactantius* * gives of her. Flora,
*having gain'd a great Eſtate by proſtituting her Body, at her Death left the
People of* Rome *her Heir, and allotted ſuch a certain ſum of Money; the
Yearly uſe of which ſhould be expended in the Celebration of her Birth-Day
with ſeveral Sports call'd* Floralia. *Which ſeeming a flagitious thing
to the Senate, they took occaſion, from the very name of the Sports* Floralia, *to add ſome Dignity to ſo ſhameful a buſineſs, to feign a Goddeſs*
Flora, *who had the care of Flowers, whom they ſhou'd Yearly appeaſe
for the greater plenty of their Corn, Vines,* &c. Her various-colour'd
Habit, with the reaſon of it, is mention'd by Ovid[1],

Cur tamen, ut dantur veſtes Cerealibus albæ,

Sic eſt hæc cultu verſicolore decens ?

An quia maturis albeſcit meſsis ariſtis ?

Et color, & ſpecies floribus omnis ineſt ?

Annuit.——

In white at *Ceres* Feaſts why are they dreſt,

While *Flora* wears a party-colour'd Veſt?

Is it becauſe Corn looks in Harveſt white,

Whilſt Flowers in various Colours take delight?

She was crown'd with Flowers, as we finde in theſe following Verſes,

Annuit : & motis flores cecidére capillis,

Decidere in menſas ut roſa miſſa ſolet.

She

She nods : and Flowers fell from her Head,
Like Roſes on a Table ſhed.

Anſwerable to the Life of the Authour were the Sports on her Fe-
ſtival ; laſcivious, and celebrated by laſcivious Perſons. O V I D *, * Ibid.

Quærere conabar quare laſcivia major
His foret in ludis, liberiórque jocus, &c.
Turba quidem cur hos celebret meretricia ludos.

I did enquire why a more wanton way
Theſe Sports are granted, and a freer Play :
Why Proſtitutes ſhould at theſe Rites attend.

Which Cato had no ſooner entered, but his Gravity forc'd him to retire.
M A R T I A L,

Nôſſes jocoſæ dulce cùm ſacrum Floræ,
Feſtósque luſus, & licentiam vulgi,
Cur in Theatrum Cato ſevere veniſti?
An ideò tantùm veneras, ut exires?

Thou knew'ſt, that Flora's joyful Rites
Free Licence had, and all Delights ;
Why cam'ſt thou Cato to the Play?
Cam'ſt onely thou to go away?

Which Story is more copiouſly related by Valerius Maximus. Onu-
phrius Panvinius mentions a Coyn , in which we have the firſt, that
cauſed theſe Sports to be celebrated. C. MEMMIUS FLO-
RALIA PRIMUS FECIT. She had her Flamen, mention'd
by Varro[1]. [1] De Leg. La.

" Oppoſite to this , on the North-ſide, the Goddeſs POMONA
" crown'd with a Garland of ſeveral Fruits; in her right Hand, a Pru-
" ning-Hook ; in her left Hand, the Sun : at her Feet, all ſorts of Graffing,
" and Gardening-Tools.
                                                                    OVID;

* Metam.
lib.xiv. Fab.
16.

OVID * thus deſcribes her at large,

Rege ſub hoc POMONA *fuit : quà nulla* Latinas
Inter Hamadryadas *coluit ſolertiùs hortos :*
Nec ſuit arborei ſtudioſior altera fœtûs ;
Unde tenet nomen. Non ſylvas illa, nec amnes,
Rus amat, & ramos felicia poma ſerentes.
Nec jaculo gravis eſt, ſed aduncâ dextera falce :
Quà modò luxuriem premit, & ſpatiantia paſsim
Brachia compeſcit : fiſſo modò cortice, lignum
Inſerit, & ſuccos alieno praſtat alumno.
Nec ſentire ſitim patitur, bibulæque recurvas
Radicis fibras labentibus irrigat undis.

POMONA flouriſh'd in thoſe times of eaſe:
Of all the *Latian Hamadryades,*
None fruitful Hort-yards held in more repute,
Or took more care to propagate their Fruit;
Thereof ſo nam'd. Nor Streams, nor ſhady Groves,
But Trees producing gen'rous Burdens loves.
Her Hand a Hook, and not an Jav'lin bare :
Now prunes luxurious Twigs, and Boughs, that dare
Tranſcend their Bounds : now ſlits the Bark, the Bud
Inſerts, enforc'd to nurſe anothers Brood.
Nor ſuffers them to ſuffer Thirſt, but brings
To moiſture-ſucking Roots ſoft ſliding Springs.

She had her *Flamen* too, though the laſt of the fifteen. SEXTUS
POMPEIUS, *Maximæ dignationis* Flamen *Dialis eſt inter* XV.
Flamines: *& quum cæteri diſcrimina Majeſtatis ſuæ habeant, minimi habe-*
tur Pomonalis; *quòd* Pomona *leviſsimo fructui agrorum præſidet.* The
Flamen *of* Jupiter *is of the greateſt Dignity amongſt the fifteen Flamens.*
There is a diſtinction betwixt all of them, but the meaneſt is the Flamen of
Pomona, *becauſe ſhe preſides over the meaneſt Fruit of the Grounds.*

BORNAS,

"BOREAS, *inſtead of Feet, two Serpents Tails, his Wings covered*
" *with Snow; his Emblem, a rockie Mountainous Country, and the* Pleiades
" *riſing over it ; his Motto,*

      ——SCYTHIAM SEPTEMQUE TRIONES
HORRIFER INVADIT——

That the Antients deſcribed BOREAS with Serpents Tails, in-
ſtead of Feet, appears out of PAUSANIAS[*], Ἐξ ἀισπερῆ μεδϊῆι Βορέαι ἐςῶ   [*] In Eliacis.
ἁρπαζῶι Ὀρεθυιαν. Ὀυραί δὲ ὄφεων ἀυτῷ ἀνδϊῆ είσι ἀντῶι *If you compaſs it on the left*
Hand, there is Boreas *forcibly taking away* Orithyia: *He hath* Serpents
Tails inſtead of Feet.

Thus OVID deſcribes him ſtealing away *Orithyia,*

   Hæc Boreas, *aut his non inferiora loquutus,*
   Excuſſit pennas : quarum jactatibus omnis
   Afflata eſt tellus, latiſmque perhorruit æquor.
   Pulvereámque trahens per ſumma cacumina pallam,
   Verrit humum, pavidámque metu caligine tectus
   Orithyiam *adamans fulvis complectitur alis.*

   Thus *Boreas* chafes, or no leſs ſtorming, ſhook
   His horrid Wings ; whoſe aiery motion ſtrook
   The Earth with Blaſts, and made the Ocean roar,
   Trailing his duſty Mantle on the Floor.
   He hid himſelf in Clouds of Duſt, and caught
   Belov'd *Orithyia,* with her fear diſtraught.

VIRGIL[†],   [†] Georgic.

   Qualis Hyperboreis *Aquilo cùm denſus ab oris*
   Incubuit, Scythiæque *hyemes, atque arida differt*
   Nubila.——

   As when from *Hyperborean* Mountains fierce
   Boreas doth Clouds, and *Scythian* Storms diſperſe.

                        CLAUDIAN,

* De rapu
Proserp.
lib. i.
Claudian*,

> ———————— ceu turbine rauco
> Cùm gravis armatur Boreas, glaciéque nivali
> Hispidus, & Geticà concretus grandine pennas,
> Bella cupit, pelagus, sylvas, campósque sonoro
> Flamine rapturus.———

As with a Whirl-Winde when rough Boreas arms
Wings stiff with Ice, and Snow, and Gothick Storms,
Desiring War, the Woods, and Deeps profound,
And Plains breaks thorough with a dreadful sound.

"Auster, in a dark-coloured Habit, with Wings like Clouds; his
" Embleme, a Cloudy Sky, and Showers: his Motto,

NUBIBUS ASSIDUIS PLUVIAQVE MADESCIT.

The Authours of Natural History do attribute a Thunder-Bolt to
the South-Winde alone. From whence Virgil, describing Vulcan's
Shop,

> His informatum manibus, jam parte politâ
> Fulmen erat, toto Genitor quæ plurima cœlo
> Dejicit in terras: pars imperfecta manebat.
> Tres imbris torti radios, tres nubis aquosæ
> Addiderant, rutili tres ignis, & alitis Austri.

A Thunder-Bolt half finish'd now in hand,
(Many of these by angry Jove are thrown
From Heav'n to Earth) the rest as yet not done.
Three parts of Hail, three of a Wat'ry Cloud,
As much of Fire, and three of Winde allow'd.

Upon which place Servius. Nonnulli manubias Fulminis his
Numinibus, Jovi, Junoni, Marti, & Austro vento afferunt attribui,
quod ex hoc Maronis loco ostendunt,   Of this Winde we have the Pi-
                                        cture

cture in *Antoninus's* Pillar at *Rome*, remarkable for the History, in which is represented the Rain, that fell in the Tents of the *Romans*, ready to perish for Drouth, and the Thunder, and Lightning, which at the same time destroyed the Enemy: obtain'd by the Prayers of a *Christian Legion*, as the *Fathers* of those times relate it; by others attributed either to the Piety of the Emperour, or the Magick of *Arnuphis*: of which CLAUDIAN;

> *Laute tibi nulla Ducum; nam flammeus imber in hostem*
> *Decidit : hunc dorso trepidum flammante ferebat*
> *Ambustus sonipes ; hic tabescente soluta*
> *Subsedit galeâ, liquefactâque pulvere cuspis*
> *Conduit, & subitis fluxère liquoribus enses.*
> *Tunc contenta polo, mortalis nescia teli,*
> *Pugna fuit. Chaldæa mago seu carmina ritu*
> *Armavère Deos; seu, quod reor, omne Tonantis*
> *Obsequium* Marci *mores potuère mereri.*

> The Chiefs no Fame got there; the Enemie's force
> A fiery Show'r dispers'd : a burning Horse
> Bore this on's flaming Back; this over-turn'd,
> His Cask did melt, in Dust his Jav'lin burn'd,
> And melting Swords in smoaking Rivers glide.
> Heaven's Arcenal did for this Fight provide
> Weapons destroying more then Mortal Arms.
> Either the Gods were arm'd by Magick Charms,
> Or *Jove* so much to *Marcus* merits ow'd,
> That all this kindness he on him bestow'd.

It is thus described by D I O. *You might see at the same time Rain of Fire fall from Heaven : some were wet, and drank; others were burnt, and died. The Fire touch'd not the* Romans; *if it fell among them, it was immediatly quench'd. The Rain did their Adversaries no good, but rather being Oil increased the flame. They sought for Water, while the Rain fell on them. Some of them wounded themselves, as if they meant to quench the*

Z   *Fire*

Fire with their Blood ; others ran *over to the* Romans,   *who alone had the
Water could save them* ; *and those* Antoninus *sav'd.* The same Authour,
who liv'd in the time of *Commodus,* Son to *Antoninus,* mentions, from a
Report in his time, the Magick of *Arnuphis,* as a cause of it, as it is deliver'd by *Xiphiline,* Patriarch of *Constantinople :* *'Tis reported, that* Arnuphis, *an* Ægyptian *Magician ,   then in company of the Emperour* Mar-
cus Antoninus, *had invoked with his Magick Art, among other Gods, the
aerial* Mercury, *by whose assistance he obtain'd the Showr.*   And thus the
Story is told by S U I D A S *.   Others mention *Julian* the Magician.
The *Christians* had a fair Plea for what they pretended, an acknow-
ledgment from the Emperour himself, by Letter to the Senate ,   had
not that Letter, still remaining, upon examination prov'd counterfeit.
The Picture, being rare, we have caused here to be publish'd.

Baronius mistook it for *Jupiter Pluvius* , who is never represented
with Wings. This Winde is excellently describ'd by O V I D ',

——————— *madidis* Notus *evolat alis,*
Terribilem piceâ tectus caligine vultum ;

                                                          Barba

Barba gravis nimbis, canis fluit unda capillis,
Fronte sedent nebulæ, rorant pennæque sinúsque.

With moist Wings *Notus* flies in sable Bags
His sowre Face hid, his Beard with Tempest sags,
His Hair sheds Crystal Drops, dark Clouds encamp
Upon his Brows, his Wings and Bosom damp.

His Thunder-Bolt is mention'd too by *Lucretius* ;

Altitonans Volturnus, *&* Auster *ulmine pollens.*

" ZEPHYRUS, *like an* Adonis *with Wings* ; *the Emblem, a Flow-*
" *ery Plain* ; *the Word,*

——TEPENTIBUS AURIS
DEMULCET——

So CLAUDIAN describes*,   * De rapu Proserp. lib. ii.

——*Pater ò gratissime Veris,*
Qui mea lascivo regnas per prata volatu
Semper, & assiduis irroras flatibus annum, &c.
—— *ille novo madidantes nectare pennas*
Concutit, & glebas fæcundo rore maritat,
Quáque volat, vernus sequitur color : omnia in herbas
Turget humus, medióque patent convexa sereno.
Sanguineo splendore rosas, vaccinia nigro
Induit, & dulci violas ferrugine pingit.

Bless'd Father of the Spring, all Hail,
Who rul'st my Meadows with a wanton Gale,
And dew'st the Season with a constant breeze, *&c.*
From his moist Wings he richest *Nectar* sheds,
And the hard Glebe with pregnant Moisture weds :
Colour the Spring attends, and every where
Earth swells with Herbage, Heav'n's high Fore-head clear.

> Rofes in Red, Berries in Black he dies,
> And gives the Violets Purple Liveries.

LUCRETIUS calls it *the Meſſenger of* Venus:

> *Et ver, & Venus, & Veneris prænuntius antè*
> *Pennatus graditur* Zephyrus *veſtigia propter.*

> The Spring, and *Venus,* warming *Zephyre* brings
> Love's gentle Herbinger on painted Wings.

† Imag. PHILOSTRATUS, repreſents it thus, *A Youth ſmooth-fac'd, with Wings on his Shoulders, and on his Head a Garland of ſeveral Flowers.*

* In Hercule SENECA*,
O. tœi.

> ——— *quæ* Zephyro
> *Subdita tellus, ſtupet aurato*
> *Flumine clarum radiare* Tagum.

> The Lands, where *Zephyre* dwells, behold
> With wonder *Tagus* ſhine in Gold.

† In laudibus CLAUDIAN[†],
Siriue.

> *Deſeritur jam ripa* Tagi, Zephyríque *reliĉis*
> *Sedibus,* Aurorǽ *famulas properatur ad urbes.*

> He *Tagus* banks, and *Zephyr's* Court forſakes,
> And haſte to Conquer'd *Eaſtern* Cities makes.

Not ſo much from the Vernal temperature of the place, as that it was eſteem'd the remoteſt place from whence *Italy* received theſe *We-ſtern* Gales.

> "*The great Figure on the top of all repreſents* PLENTY, *crowned, a*
> "*Branch of Palm in her right Hand, a* Cornu-copiæ *in her left.*

The

The Muſick aloft on both ſides, and on the two Balconies within, were twelve Waits, ſix Trumpets, and three Drums.

At a convenient diſtance before this Structure, were two Stages erected, divided, planted, and adorned like Gardens, each of them eight Yards in length, five in breadth. Upon that on the *North*-ſide ſate a Woman repreſenting PLENTY, crowned with a Garland of divers Flowers, clad in a Green Veſtment embroidered with Gold, holding a *Cornu-copiæ* : her Attendants, two Virgins.

At His Majeſtie's approach to the *Arch*, this Perſon repreſenting PLENTY roſe up, and made Addreſs to him in theſe Words ;

> *Great Sir, the Star, which at Your Happy Birth*
> *Joy'd with his Beams (at Noon) the wond'ring Earth,*
> *Did with auſpicious luſtre, then, preſage*
> *The glitt'ring Plenty of this Golden Age ;*
> *The Clouds blown o're, which long our joys o'recaſt,*
> *And the ſad Winter of Your abſence paſt,*
> *See ! the three ſmiling Seaſons of the Year*
> *Agree at once to bid You Welcome here ;*
> *Her Homage Dutious Flora comes to pay ;*
> *With Her Enamel'd Treaſure ſtrows Your Way :*
> *Ceres, and Pales, with a bounteous Hand,*
> *Diffuſe their Plenty over all Your Land ;*
> *And Bacchus is ſo laviſh of his Store,*
> *That Wine flows now, where Water ran before.*
> *Thus Seaſons, Men, and Gods their Joy expreſs ;*
> *To ſee Your Triumph, and our Happineſs.*

His Majeſty, having paſſed the four *Triumphal Arches*, was, at TEMPLE-Bar, entertained with the View of a delightful Boſcage, full of ſeveral Beaſts, both Tame, and Savage, as alſo ſeveral living Figures, and Muſick of eight Waits. But this, being the Limit of the Citie's Liberty, muſt be ſo likewiſe of our Deſcription.

A BRIEF

NARRATIVE

OF HIS

MAJESTIE'S

SOLEMN CORONATION:

WITH

His Magnificent PROCEEDING, and

ROYAL FEAST in

WESTMINSTER-HALL.

A BRIEF
NARRATIVE
Of
His Majestie's Solemn Coronation.

Pon the 23d of *April*, being Saint *George's* Day, about seven in the Morning, the *King* took Water from the *Privy-Stairs* at *White-Hall*, and landed at the *Parliament-Stairs*: from whence He went up to the Room behind the *Lords-House*, called the *Prince's Lodgings*: where, after He had reposed Himself for a while, He was arayed in Royal Robes of Crimson Velvet, furr'd with Ermine: By which time the *Nobility*, being come together in the *Lords-House*, and *Painted-Chamber*, Robed themselves.

The *Judges* also, with those of the *Long-Robe*, the *Knights* of the *Bath* (then in their Robes of Purple Satin, lined with white Taffaty) and *Gentlemen* of the *Privy-Chamber*, met in the Court of *Requests*. And, after some space, being drawn down into *Westminster-Hall*, where this great Solemnity (ordered by the Officers at Arms) began; the *Nobility*, in their proper Robes, carrying their Coronets in their Hands, proceeded according to their several Dignities, and Degrees, before His *Majesty*, up to His Throne of State; which was raised at the *West* end of that large and noble Room, and there placed themselves upon each side thereof.

A a 2

The

The *King* being thus set in a rich Chair, under a glorious Cloth of State, Sir *Gilbert Talbot* K.t, *Master* of the *Jewel-House*, presented the *Sword of State*, as also the *Sword* called *Curtana*, and two other *Swords*, to the *Lord High-Constable* ; who took and delivered them to the *Lord High-Chamberlain*, and he laid them upon the Table before the *King*.

Then did he also deliver the *Spurs* to the *Lord High-Constable*; and he the same to the *Lord High-Chamberlain*, who also placed them upon the Table.

Immediately after the *Dean* and *Prebends* of *Westminster*, (by whom the *Regalia* had been brought in Procession from the *Abbey-Church* unto *Westminster-Hall*) being vested in rich Copes, came up from the lower end thereof, in manner following.

1. The *Serjeant* of the *Vestry*, in a Scarlet Mantle.
2. Then the *Children* of the *King's Chapel*, in Scarlet Mantles.
3. Then the *Quire* of *Westminster*, in Surplices.
4. Then the *Gentlemen* of the *King's Chapel*, in Scarlet Mantles.
5. Next the *Pursuivants*, *Heralds*, and *Provincial* Kings of Arms.
6. Then the *Dean*, carrying Saint *Edward's Crown*.

And after him five of the *Prebends* of that Church; the first carrying the *Sceptre* with the *Cross*.

The second the *Sceptre* with the *Dove*.

The third the *Orb* with the *Cross*.

The fourth King *Edward's Staff*.

The fifth the *Chalice* and *Patens*.

Passing thus through the *Hall*, and making their due Reverences in three places thereof; the *Quires*, with the Officers at Arms falling off on each side, towards the upper end of the Room; the said *Dean* and *Prebends* ascended the Steps; at the top whereof *Garter*, Principal King of *Arms* standing, conducted them to the *Table* placed before the *Throne*, where they made their last Reverence.

Which being done, the *Dean* first presented the *Crown*, which was by the *Lord High Constable*, and *Lord Great-Chamberlain*, set upon the Table; who likewise afterwards received from each of the *Prebends* that part of the *Regalia*, which they carried, and laid them also by the *Crown* : which done, they retired.

Then

Then, the *Lord Great-Chamberlain* presenting the *Regalia* severally to the *King*, His *Majesty* thereupon disposed of them unto the *Noble-men* hereafter named, to be carried by them in the *Proceeding* to the *Abbey-Church*, viz.

Saint *Edward's Staff* to the *Earl* of *Sandwich*.

The *Spurs* to the *Earl* of *Pembroke* and *Montgomery*.

The *Sceptre* with the *Cross* to the *Earl* of *Bedford*.

The *Pointed Sword* (born on the left hand of *Curtana*) to the *Earl* of *Derby*.

The *Pointed Sword* (born on the right hand thereof) to the *Earl* of *Shrewsbury*.

The *Sword* called *Curtana* to the *Earl* of *Oxford*.

The *Sword* of *State* to the *Earl* of *Manchester*.

The *Sceptre* with the *Dove* to the *Duke* of *Albe-marle*.

The *Orb* with the *Cross* to the *Duke* of *Buckingham*.

Saint *Edward's Crown* to the *Duke* of *Ormond*.

The *Patena* to the *Bishop* of *Exeter* ; and lastly,

The *Chalice* to the *Bishop* of *London*.

All things being thus prepared , (it being about ten a Clock,) the *Proceeding* began from the *Hall* into the *Palace-Yard*, through the *Gate-House*, and the end of *King's-street* ; thence along the *Great Sanctuary*, and so to the *West-end* of the *Abbey-Church*, all upon Blew Cloth, which was spread upon the Ground, from the *Throne* in *Westminster-Hall* to the great Steps in the same *Abbey-Church*, by Sir *George Carteret* Knight, His *Majestie's* Vice-Chamberlain, as *Almoner* for that Day by special Appointment.

The

The PROCEEDING to the CORONATION
was in this following Order.

THE *Drums* four.

The *Trumpets* sixteen, in four *Classis.*

The *Six Clerks* of the *Chancery.*

Ten of the K I N G's *Chaplains,* having Dignities.

The *Aldermen* of LONDON.

The K I N G's *Learned Council* at *Law.*

The K I N G's *Solicitour.* The K I N G's *Attorney.*

The K I N G's eldest *Serjeant* at *Law.*

The *Esquires* of the *Body.*

The *Masters* of *Request.*

The *Gentlemen* of the *Privy-Chamber.*

The *Knights* of the *Bath,* in their *Purple Robes.*

The *Barons* of the *Exchequer,* and *Justices* of both *Benches,* two and two, in order, according to their Seniority.

The *Lord Chief-Baron.* The *Lord Chief-Justice* of the *Common-Pleas.*

The *Master* of the *Rolls,* The *Lord Chief-Justice* of the *Kings-Bench.*

The *Serjeant-Porter.* The *Serjeant* of the *Vestry.*

The *Children* of the *King's Chapel.*

The *Gentlemen* of the *King's Chapel.*

The *Prebends* of *Westminster.*

The *Master* of the *Jewel-House.*

The *Knights* of the *Privy-Council.*

Port-culliss, Pursuivant at Arms.

The *Barons* in their Robes, two and two, carrying their Caps of Crimson Velvet, turn'd up with Miniver, in their Hands.

The *Bishops,* two and two, according to their Dignities, and Consecrations.

Rouge-Croix,   *Blew-Mantle,*   Pursuivants.

The *Viscounts,* two and two, in their Robes, with their Coronets in their Hands.

Somerset,   ,   *Chester,*   Heralds.

The *Earls,* two and two, in their Robes, holding their Coronets in their Hands.

Richmond,

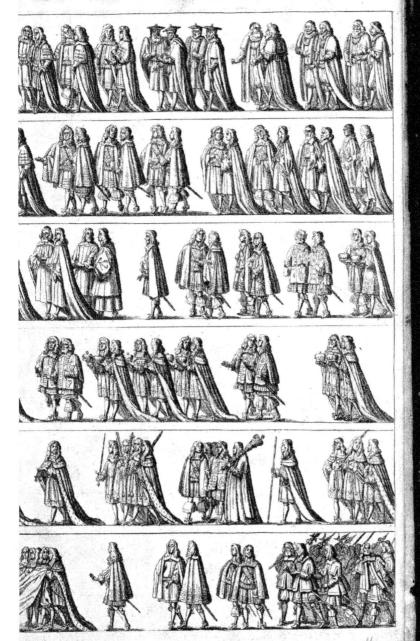

Richmond,   *Windsor,*   Heralds.
The *Marquess* of *Dorchester,*   The *Marquess* of *Worcester,*
    in their Robes, with their Coronets in their Hands.

Lancaster,   *York,*   Heralds.
Norroy,   *Clarencieux,*   Provincial King's,
    carrying their Crowns in their Hands.

The *Lord High-Treasurer,*   The *Lord High Chancellour.*

Saint *Edward's Staff,* born by the *Earl* of *Sandwich,*
The *Spurs,* born by the *Earl* of *Penbroke,* and *Montgomery,*
Saint *Edward's Sceptre,* born by the *Earl* of *Bedford.*

| The *third Sword,* drawn, and born by the *Earl* of *Derby.* | The *Sword* called *Curtana,* drawn, and born by the *Earl* of *Oxford.* | The *Pointed Sword,* drawn, and born by the *Earl* of *Shrewsbury.* |

The *Lord Maior* of   *Garter,* Principal   The *Gentleman-Usher*
    London.   King of Arms.   of the *Black-Rod.*

The *Earl* of *Lindsey,*
Lord *Great-Chamberlain* of ENGLAND.

| Arms. | The *Earl* of *Suffolk,* Earl *Marshal* for this present occasion. | The *Sword* of State in the Scabbard, born by the *Earl* of *Manchester,* Lord *Chamberlain* of the Houshold. | The *Earl* of *Northumberland,* Lord *Constable* of *England* for this present occasion. | Arms. |

His Highness the *Duke* of YORK.

| at | The *Sceptre,* with the *Dove,* born by the *Duke* of *Albemarle.* | St. *Edward's Crown,* born by the *Duke* of *Ormond,* Lord *High-Steward* for this present occasion. | The *Orb,* born by the *Duke* of *Buckingham.* | at |

| Serjeants | The *Patena,* born by the *Bishop* of *Exeter* in his *Cope.* | The *Regale,* or *Chalice,* born by the *Bishop* of *London* in his *Cope.* | Serjeants |

The

The Pensioners with their Pole-Axes.

Barons of the Cinque-Ports, (their whole Number XVI.) habited in Doublets of Crimson Satin, Scarlet Hose, Scarlet Gowns, lined with Crimson Satin, black Velvet Caps, and black Velvet Shoes, carrying the *Canopy*.

The KING supported by the Bishops of *Bath* and *Wells*, and *Duresme*.

His Train born by the Lords *Mandevil*, *Cavendish*, *Ossory*, and *Percy*; and assisted by the Lord *Mansfield*, Master of the *Robes*.

The *Earl* of *Lauderdale*, one of the *Gentlemen* of the *Bed-Chamber*.

Mr. *Seamour*, Mr. *Ashburnham*, both Grooms of the Bed-Chamber.

The *Captain* of the *Guard*.

The *Captain* of the *Pensioners*.

The *Yeomen* of *Guard*, in their *Coats*.

Barons of the Cinque-Ports, (their whole Number XVI.) habited in Doublets of Crimson Satin, Scarlet Hose, Scarlet Gowns, lined with Crimson Satin, black Velvet Caps, and black Velvet Shoes, carrying the *Canopy*.

The *Pensioners* with their *Pole-Axes*.

When the *Proceeding* was entered the *Abbey-Church*, all, passing through the *Quire*, went up the Stairs toward the *great Theatre*; and, as they came to the top thereof, were disposed by the *Heralds* into two *Galleries*, built on either side the upper end of the *Quire*. On the *North* side, the *Aldermen* of *London*, the *Judges*, and others of the *Long-Robe*; as also the *Quire* of *Westminster*, with the *Gentlemen* and *Children* of the *King's Chapel*; and, on the *South* side, the *Knights* of the *Bath*, and *Gentlemen* of the *Privy-Chamber*.

Near the *Pulpit* stood the *Master* of the *Jewel-House*, and the *Lord Maior* of *London*.

The *Nobility* were seated on Forms round about the in-side of the *Theater*: on the corner whereof, nearest to the *Altar*, adjoyning to the two uppermost *Pillars*, stood the *Provincial Kings*, *Heralds*, and

and *Purſuivants* at Arms, within Rails there placed.

Within the Rails, on either ſide the entrance of the *Theatre* from the *Quire*, ſtood the Serjeants at Arms (XVI. in number) with their Maces. And over the Door, at the *Weſt* end of the *Quire*, ſtood the Drums and Trumpets.

The *King*, being entered the *Weſt-*door of the *Church* (within which a *Fald-ſtool*, and *Cuſhions* were laid ready for him to kneel at) was received with an *Anthem*, begun by the whole *Quire*, viz.

The firſt, fourth, fifth, and ſixth *Verſes* of the 122d *Pſalm* : beginning thus;

> *I was glad when they ſaid unto me , We will go into the Houſe of the Lord*, &c.

He kneeled down, and uſed ſome ſhort Ejaculations; which being finiſhed, He thence proceeded up to the *Theatre* (erected cloſe to the four high *Pillars*, ſtanding between the *Quire* and the *Altar*) upon which the *Throne* of *Eſtate* was placed (being a Square raiſed five Degrees) on the *Eaſt-*ſide whereof were ſet a *Chair*, *Foot-ſtool*, and *Cuſhion*, covered with Cloth of Gold, whereon for a while He repoſed Himſelf.

Immediately after, the *Biſhop* of *London* (who was appointed to Officiate, in part, that Day, for the *Arch Biſhop* of *Canterbury*, whoſe age and weakneſs rendered him uncapable of performing his whole Duty at this *Coronation*) having the *Lord High Conſtable*, the *Earl Marſhal*, the *Lord Great Chamberlain*, the *Lord High Chancellour*, and *Lord Chamberlain* of the *Houſhold* before him, went firſt to the *South*, next to the *Weſt*, and laſtly, to the *North* ſide of the *Theatre*; and at every of the ſaid three ſides, acquainted the *People*, that he preſented to them *King* CHARLES, the rightful Inheritour of the *Crown* of this *Realm*; and asked them, if they were willing to do their *Homage*, *Service*, and *Bounden Duty* to Him.

As this was doing, the *King* roſe up, and ſtood by the aforeſaid *Chair*, turning His Face ſtill to that ſide of the *Stage*, where the ſaid *Biſhop* ſtood, when he ſpake to the *People*; who ſignified their willingneſs, by loud Shouts, and Acclamations.

The ſame Queſtion was likewiſe put by the ſaid *Biſhop* to all the *Nobility* preſent.

Immediately after, this following *Anthem* was ſung by the *Gentlemen* of the *King's Chapel* :

Let thy Hand be strengthened, and thy right Hand be exalted, &c.

In which time, a large *Carpet* was spread by certain Officers of the removing *Wardrobe*, from the *Altar*, down below the *hault-Paces* thereof; and over that a *silk Carpet*, and *Cushion*, laid by the *Gentleman-Usher* of the *Black-Rod*, assisted by the *Yeoman* of the *Wardrobe*. Which being done, the *Bishop* of *London* went down from the *Theatre* towards the *Altar*; and, having made his Reverence, placed himself at the *North*-side thereof.

Then the *King* descended from His *Throne*, and proceeded towards the *Altar*, supported by the *Bishops* of *Duresme*, and *Bath* and *Wells*, with the *four Swords*; the *grand Officers*, the *Noble-men*, *Bishops*, who carried the *Regalia* before Him, and *Dean* of *Westminster* also attending. Being come to the Steps of the *Altar*, He kneeled down, and first offered a *Pall* of Cloth of Gold; next an *Ingot* of Gold of a pound weight, prepared by the Master of the great *Wardrobe*, and *Treasurer* of the *Houshold*, by virtue of their *Offices*. Immediately after, His *Majestie* retired to a *Chair of State*, set on the *South*-side of the *Altar*, a little below the Traverse of Crimson Taffaty.

After this, the *Bishops*, and *Noble-men*, who carried the *Regalia*, presented every particular to the *Bishop* of *London*, who placed them upon the *Altar*; and then retired to their Seats. And the *King* kneeled at a *Fald-stool* (set on the right side of his said *Chair of State*) whil'st the *Bishop* of *London* said the *Prayer*, beginning thus,

O God, which dost visit those, that are humble, &c.

Which *Prayer* ended, the *Bishop* of *Worcester* went up into the *Pulpit*, placed on the *North*-side of the *Altar*, opposite to the *King*, and began his S E R M O N; the Text being taken out of the 28th *Chapter* of the *Proverbs*, and the second *Verse*.

On the *King*'s right Hand stood the *Bishop* of *Duresme*, and beyond him the *Noble-men*, that carried the S V V O R D S, who held them naked, and erect. The *Duke* of Y O R K sate a little behind Him on His left Hand; next to whom stood the *Bishop* of *Bath* and *Wells*, together with the *Lord Great-Chamberlain*.

The

The *Lord High-Chancellour*, and *Lord High-Treafurer*, fate on a Form behind the *Duke* of YORK; and behind them, in a Gallery, fate the *Dutchefs* of YORK.

In the fame Gallery alfo were placed

    Baron Bateville, Ordinary *Ambaffadour* from *Spain*.

    Prince Maurice of *Naffau*, Extra-ordinary *Ambaffadour* from the *Electour* of *Brandenburgh*.

    Monfieur Weyman, the *Electour's Chancellour*, who was joyned in Commiffion with him.

    The *Count Coningsmark*, Envoy from *Sweden*.

    Monfieur Friefendorf, Refident of *Sweden*.

    Monfieur Petcom, Refident of *Denmark*.

    Monfieur Pleffis Bellieure, Envoy from *Monfieur* the *Duke* of *Orleans*.

    Signieur Giavarina, Refident of *Venice*.

    Signieur Bernardi, Refident of *Genoa*.

    Monfieur La-Motte,
    and } Envoys from the *Prince Electour*.
    Monfieur Frays,

    Monfieur Gormers, Deputy Extra-ordinary from *Hamburgh*.

    An Envoy from the *Cardinal of Hefs*.

    The *Marquefs de Montbrun*, with feveral other *Gentlemen-ftrangers*.

But *Don Francifco de Mello*, the *Ambaffadour* of *Portugal*, was placed in the *Lord Chamberlain's* Box.

On the *North*-fide of the *Altar* fate the *Bifhop* of *London*, directly oppofite to the *King* in the *Arch-Bifhop's* Chair, covered with Purple Velvet : the reft of the *Bifhops* being placed on Forms behind him.

And higher, towards Saint *Edward's Chapel*, ftood *Garter*, Principal King of Arms, with the *Officers* of the ftanding and moving *Wardrobe*, in Scarlet Gowns; the *Sergeant* of the *Veftry* with his gilt Verge, and other Vergers : as alfo fome of the *Grooms* and *Pages* of the *Bed-Chamber*, who attended to do fervice, as occafion required.

Oppofite to them, on the *South*-fide of the *Altar*, ftood the *Dean* and *Prebends* of *Weftminfter*.

Saint *Edward's* antient *Chair* (covered all over with Cloth of Gold) was placed upon the *North*-fide of the *Altar*, a little lower then that belonging to the *Arch-Bifhop*, but fomething nearer the middle of the *Ifle*, and between the *King's* Chair of State, and the Pulpit.

B b 2   SERMON

SERMON being ended, the *Bishop* of *London* arifing from his Seat, drew near to the *Chair* of *State*, and asked of the *King* (who then uncovered His Head) whether He was willing to take the ufual *Oath* of His *Progenitors*, *viz.* to confirm the *Laws* to the *People*, and namely the *Franchifes* granted to the *Clergy* by Saint *Edward* the *Confeffour*; to maintain the *Gofpel* eftablifhed in the *Kingdom*; to keep *Peace*; execute *Juftice*, and grant the *Commons* their rightful *Cuftoms*: unto every of which Queftions His Majefty made particular Anfwers, That *He would*.

Then likewife did the *Bifhop* of *Rocheſter* read the *Bifhop's Petition* to the *King*; the *Prayer* whereof was, That He would preferve unto them, and the *Churches* committed to their charge, all *Canonical Privileges*; due *Law*, and *Juftice*; as alfo protect, and defend *them*, and the *Churches*, under their Government: which His *Majefty* moft gracioufly by a large Anfwer (which repeated the words of the *Petition*) granted, and promifed to perform.

Afterwards the *King*, afsifted by the *Bifhops* of *Durefme*, and *Bath* and *Wells*, was led from His *Chair* up to the *Altar* (the *Sword* of *State* being born before Him, and the *Lord Great Chamberlain* attending) where He took an *Oath* to perform, and keep what He had promifed.

Which *Oath* taken, the *King* was led, in like manner, back to His *Chair* of *State*; and immediately the *Bifhop* of *London* begun the *Hymn*, *Come Holy Ghoft, eternal God*, &c. the *Quires* finging the reft of it.

And a little before the ending thereof, the *Fald-ftool* was fet again at the *King's* right Hand; whereat (as foon as the *Hymn* was finifhed) He kneeled) the *Bifhop* of *London* ftanding before Him, and faying the following *Prayer*,

We befeech thee, O Lord, Holy Father, Almighty, and everlafting God, for this thy Servant CHARLES, &c.

This *Prayer* ended, the *Bifhop* of *London* went to the *North-*fide of the *Altar*, the *King* ftill kneeling; and forthwith the *Bifhops* of *Peterborough*, and *Gloucefter*, went, and kneeled on the upper haultpace of the *Altar*, where they began the *Letany*, the *Quires* finging the *Refponfes*; the *Dean* of *Weftminfter*, kneeling all the while on the *King's* left Hand.

After the *Letany* followed three *Prayers*, faid by the *Bifhop* of *London*

London at the *North* fide of the *Altar* ; and, a little before the laft of them was ended, the *Arch-Bifhop* of *Canterbury* came out at the *North*-door of *Saint* E D W A R D's *Chapel*, vefted in a rich antient *Cope*.

The third *Prayer* being ended, the faid *Arch-Bifhop* ftanding before the *Altar*, began the *Verficle*,

> *Lift up your Hearts.*

Refp.

> *We lift them up to the Lord.*

Arch-Bifhop.

> *Let us give thanks unto the Lord our God.*

Refp.

> *It is meet and right fo to do.*

Arch-Bifhop.

> *It is very meet, and right, and our bounden Duty, that we fhould at all times, and in all places, give thanks unto thee, O Lord, Holy Father,* &c.

Then the *King* arofe from before the *Fald-ftool,* and went to the *Altar,* fupported by the aforefaid *Bifhops* of *Durefne,* and *Bath* and *Wells* : where He was difrobed by the *Lord Great-Chamberlain* of His *Royal Robes* , which were immediately carried thence into the Traverfe erected in Saint *Edward's Chapel,*

Whilft this was in doing, the *Chair,* that was before placed at the entrance of the *Theatre* was removed, and fet on the *North*-fide of the *Altar,* betwixt it, and Saint *Edward's Chair* : whereunto the *King* being come, fate down, and was *anointed* by the faid *Arch-Bifhop,* (the *Dean* of *Wefhminfter* holding the *Ampulla,* and pouring the *Oyl* out into the *Spoon*) firft on the Palms of both His Hands , the *Arch-Bifhop,* as he *anointed* Him, pronouncing the *Prayer,* which beginneth thus ;

> *Let thefe Hands be anointed with Holy Oyl , as Kings and Prophets have been anointed,* &c.

After

After which, the *Quire* sung this *Anthem*,

> Sadoc *the Priest*, *and* Nathan *the Prophet anointed* Solomon
> *King*, *and all the People rejoyced*, *and said*, God save the
> K I N G.

At the end of which *Anthem*, the *Arch-Bishop* said the *Prayer*,
beginning thus ;

> *Look down, Almighty God, with thy favourable Countenance upon this*
> *Glorious* K I N G, *&c.*

And then proceeded with His anointing on the *King's* Breaft, between His Shoulders, on both His Shoulders; the two bowings of
His Arms, and on the Crown of His Head, in manner aforefaid.

Which being done, and the *Anointing* dryed up with fine Linen;
and alfo the Loops of His Shirt clofed up by the *Dean* of *Weftminfter*,
the *Arch-Bishop* said the two *Prayers*, beginning thus ;

> 1 *God, the Son of God*, Chrift Jefus *our Lord*, *who is anointed of*
> *his Father with the Oyl of Gladnefs above his Fellows*, &c.
> 2 *God, which art the Glory of the Righteous, and the Mercy of Sin-*
> *ners*, &c.

During the time of this His *Unction*, a rich *Pall* of Cloth of Gold,
was held over the *King's* Head by the *Dukes* of *Buckingham*, and
Albe-marle; and the *Earls* of *Berks* and *Sandwich*, as *Knights* of the
moft Noble Order of the *Garter*.

After thefe *Prayers*, the *Lord Great-Chamberlain* delivered the
Coif to the *Arch-Bishop*, who put it on the *King's* Head : and immediately after, the *Dean* of *Weftminfter* put the *Colobium Sindonis*, or
Surplice upon the *King*; the *Arch-Bishop* faying the *Prayer*, beginning thus ;

> *O God, the King of Kings, and Lord of Lords, by whom Kings do*
> *reign, and Law-givers do make good Laws, vouchfafe, we befeech*
> *thee, in thy favour, to blefs this Kingly Ornament*, &c.

Then the *Dean* of *Weftminfter*, having likewife fetched the *Tiffue-*
Hofe and *Sandals* from the *Altar*, arrayed the *King* therewith ; as alfo
with the *Super-tunica*, or *clofe Pall* of Cloth of Gold, and girded the
fame about Him.

After

After all this, the said *Dean* took the *Spurs* from off the *Altar*, and delivered them to the *Lord Great-Chamberlain*, who, having touched the *King*'s Heels therewith, forthwith sent them back to the *Altar*.

Then the *Arch-Bishop* received the *Sword* of *State* in the Scabbard from the *Lord-Chamberlain* of the *Houshold*, and laid it upon the *Altar*, saying the *Prayer*, beginning thus,

> *Hear our Prayers, we beseech thee, O Lord, and vouchsafe, by thy right Hand of Majesty, to bless, and sanctifie this SWORD, &c.*

This *Prayer* finished, the *Arch-Bishop*, and *Bishops* assisting, delivered the *Sword* back to the *King*, saying, *Accipe gladium per manus Episcoporum.*

Whereupon, the *Lord Great-Chamberlain* girt it about the *King*, and the *Arch-Bishop* said,

> *Receive this Kingly Sword, which is hallowed for the defence of the Holy Church, &c.*

After this, the *Dean* of *Westminster* took the * *Armil*, made of Cloth of Tissue, and put it about the *King*'s Neck, tying it to the bowings of His Arms; the *Arch-Bishop* standing before the *King*, with the *Bishop* of *London* on His right Hand, and saying,

* *Armillæ sunt in modum Stolæ, & ab utraque Scapula usque ad Compages Brachiorum crucis obtrudantur, in ipsis Compagibus laquris sericis connexæ.*

> *Receive the Armil of Sincerity, and Wisdom, &c.*

Next the *Mantle*, or open *Pall*, being made of Cloth of Gold, and lined with red Taffaty, was put upon Him by the said *Dean*; the *Arch-Bishop* likewise using the words of Signification, viz.

> *Receive this Pall, &c.*

In the next place, the *Arch-Bishop* took *Saint* E D W A R D's *Crown*, and blessed it, saying,

> *God, the Crown of the Faithful, &c.*

In

In the mean time, *Saint* EDWARD's *Chair* was removed into the middle of the *Isle*, and set right over against the *Altar*, whither the *King* went, and sat down in it: and then the *Arch-Bishop* brought *Saint* EDWARD's *Crown* from the *Altar*, and put it upon His Head.

Whereupon, all the *People*, with loud and repeated shouts, cryed, *God save the* KING; and, by a Signal then given, the great *Ordinance* from the *Tower* were also shot off.

At the ceasing of these Acclamations, the *Arch-Bishop* went on, saying,

God crown Thee with a Crown of Glory, and Righteousness, &c.

Adding thereunto the *Prayer*, beginning thus;

* At which words the King bowed His Head. *O God of Eternity,* &c. *Bless this thy Servant, who* * *boweth His Head unto thy Majestie,* &c.

After which *Prayer*, the *Arch-Bishop* read the *Confortare,*

Be strong, and of a good Courage, and observe the Commandments of the Lord, to walk in his ways, &c.

In the mean while, the *Quires* sung this *Anthem,*

The King shall rejoyce in thy strength, O Lord. Exceeding glad shall He be of thy Salvation, &c.

Upon this, the *Dukes, Marquesses, Earls,* and *Viscounts* put on their *Coronets*; the *Barons* their *Caps*: And Mr. *Garter*, and the *Provincial Kings* put on their *Coronets.*

Then the *Master* of the *Jewel-House* delivered to the *Arch-Bishop* the *Ring*, who consecrated it, saying,

Bless, O Lord, and sanctifie this Ring. &c.

After which, he put it upon the fourth Finger of the *King's* right Hand, and said,

Receive this Ring of Kingly Dignitie, and by it the Seal of Catholick Faith, &c.

And then used the *Prayer*, beginning thus;

O God,

O God, to whom belongeth all Power, and Dignity, give unto thy Servant CHARLES *the Fruit of His Dignity,* &c.

Which *Prayer* being finished, the *Linen Gloves* were delivered to the KING by the *Lord Great-Chamberlain.* Then the KING went to the *Altar*, ungirt His *Sword*, and offered it: which, being redeemed by the *Lord-Chamberlain* of the *Houshold*, was drawn out of the Scabbard, and carried naked by him all the following part of the Solemnity.

. Then the *Arch-Bishop* took the *Scepter*, with the *Cross*, from off the *Altar*, and delivered it into the KING's right Hand, saying,

Receive this Scepter, the Sign of Kingly Power, the Rod of Kingdoms, the Rod of Virtue, &c.

Whilst this was pronouncing by the *Arch-Bishop*, Mr. *Henry Howard* (Brother to *Thomas* Duke of *Norfolk*) delivered, by virtue of his Tenure of the *Manour* of *Wirksop*, in the County of *Norfolk*, to the *King* a rich *Glove* for His right Hand; which having put on, He then received the *Scepter*. And after that the *Arch-Bishop* said the *Prayer*, beginning thus,

O Lord, the Fountain of all good things, &c. *Grant, we beseech thee, to this thy Servant* CHARLES, *that He may order aright the Dignity, which He hath obtained,* &c.

During which time, the said Mr. *Howard* performed the Service, *ratione tenuræ dicti Manerii de* Wirksop, of supporting the *King's* right Arm.
Next of all, the *Arch-Bishop* took the *Scepter* with the *Dove*, and gave it into the *King's* Hand also, saying,

Receive the Rod of Vertue, and Equity, learn to make much of the Godly, and to terrifie the Wicked, &c.

After which, the *King* kneeled, holding both the *Scepters* in His Hands, whilst the *Arch-Bishop* thus blessed Him,

C c

The

The Lord bless Thee, and keep Thee ; and as He hath made Thee King over his People , so he still prosper Thee in this World, and make Thee partaker of his Eternal Felicity in the World to come. Amen.

Then the KING arose, and set Himself again in Saint *Edward's Chair,* whil'st the *Arch-Bishop* and *Bishops* present, one after another, kneeled before Him, and were kissed by Him.

Which done, the KING returned to that *Chair,* placed on the *Theatre* behind His *Throne ,* having then also the *four Swords* born naked before Him, (the *Arch Bishops, Bishops,* and *Great Officers* attending) at whose arrival there, the *Arch Bishop* said this *Prayer,*

Grant, O Lord, that the Clergie and People, gathered together by thine Ordinance for this service of the KING, &c.

Then the *King* reposed Himself in the said *Chair,* whilst both the *Quires* sung *Te Deum.*

When *Te Deum* was ended, the *King* ascended His *Throne* placed in the midst of the *Theatre* (the *Swords,* and Great *Officers* standing on either side ; as also the *Bishops*) the *Arch-Bishop* then saying,

Stand, and hold fast from henceforth that Place, whereof hitherto You have been Heir by the Succession of Your Fore-Fathers, &c.

After this, the *Bishops,* and *Nobility* did their Homage to the *King* in manner following.

And first the *Arch-Bishop* of *Canterbury* kneeled down before the *King's* Knees, and said,

I, WILLIAM Arch-Bishop *of* CANTERBURY, *shall be Faithful, and True, and Faith, and Truth bear unto You, Our Sovereign Lord, and Your Heirs, Kings of* ENGLAND, *and shall do, and truly acknowledg the Service of the Land, which I claim to hold of You, in right of the Church :* So help me God.

Which said, he kissed the *King's* left Cheek.

The like did all the other *Bishops,* that were present.

Then came up the *Duke* of YORK, with *Garter,* Principal *King* of *Arms,* before Him, and His Train born by two Gentle-men, who,
                                                                                being

being arrived at the *Throne*, kneeled down before the *King*, put off His Coronet, and did His *Homage* in these words;

I, James *Duke* of York, become *Your* Liege-man, of Life and Limb, and of Earthly Worship: and Faith and Truth I shall bear unto You, to live and die against all manner of Folk : So God me help. At which the *Drums* beat, *Trumpets* sounded, and all the *People* shouted.

The like did the *Dukes* of *Buckingham*, and *Albe-marle*, for themselves, and the rest of the *Dukes*.

So also did the *Marquesses* of *Worcester*, and *Dorchester*.

Next, the *Earl* of *Oxford* did *Homage* after the same manner for himself, and the rest of the *Earls*, who attended upon him to signifie their Consents.

After him, *Viscount Hereford* did the like for himself, and the rest of the *Viscounts* ; and then the *Drums* beat, and *Trumpets* sounded again, and the *People* shouted.

Lastly, the *Baron Audley* in like manner did *Homage* for himself, and all the *Baronage*, who also accompanied him to the *Throne*, in testification of their Consents ; which being finished, *Drums*, *Trumpets*, and *Shouts* followed.

Afterwards the *Duke* of York, and all the *Nobility* singly ascended the *Throne*, and touched the *King's Crown*, promising by that Ceremony to be ever ready to support it with all their power.

During the performing of this Solemn Ceremony, the *Lord High-Chancellour* went to the *South West*, and *North-sides* of the *Stage*, and proclaimed to the *People* the *King's General Pardon*, being attended by Mr. *Garter* to the *South-side*, and by a *Gentle-man Usher*, and two *Heralds* to the other two Sides.

And at these three Sides, at the same time, did the *Lord Cornwallis*, *Treasurer* of His *Majestie's Houshold*, fling abroad the *Medals*, both of Gold, and Silver, prepared for the Coronation, as a Princely Donation, or Largess, among the *People*. An *Ectype* of which is this,

The *King* being thus enthronized, the *Gentlemen* of His *Chapel* began this following *Anthem*,

> *Behold, O Lord, our Defender, and look upon the Face of thine Anointed.*

At the ending of which *Anthem*, the *Trumpets* founded, and *Drums* beat again. In which time the *Bishop* of *London* went up to the High-*Altar*, and began the *Communion*; and immediately the *King* took off His *Crown*, and delivered it to the *Lord High-Chamberlain* to hold; the *Scepter* with the *Crofs* to Mr. *Henry Howard*, and that with the *Dove* to the *Duke* of *Albemarle*.

The E p i s t l e (taken out of the Firſt *Epiſtle* of St. *Peter*, the ſecond *Chapter*, and beginning at the eleventh *Verſe*) was read by the *Bishop* of *Chichefter*.

The G o s p e l (being part of the twenty ſecond *Chapter* of St. *Matthew*, beginning at the fifteenth *Verſe*)by the *Bishop* of *Ely*.

After which, the *Nicene Creed* was began by the *Bishop* of *London*, and ſung by the *Gentle-men* of the *Chapel*.

All which time the *King* ſtood by His *Throne*.

But towards the end of the *Creed* He took again His *Crown* from the *Lord Great-Chamberlain*, and put it on His Head; as alſo the *Scepter* with the *Crofs* from Mr. *Howard*, and that with the *Dove* from the *Duke* of *Albemarle*, and prepared for His Deſcent from His *Throne* towards the *Altar*, to receive the Communion.

And, as ſoon as ſinging of the *Creed* was fully ended, the *King* deſcended with the *Crown* on His Head, and *Scepters* in both Hands, (the *Bishops* of *Durefm*, and *Bath* and *Wells*, ſupporting Him) with the four *Swords* naked before, all the great *Officers* attending. In the time of which *Proceeding* the *Quire* ſang,

> *Let my Prayer come up into thy prefence, as the Incenfe, and the lifting up of my Hand be as an Evening-Sacrifice.*

Here the *Arch-Bishop* of *Canterbury* retired from the *Ceremonies* into Saint *Edward's Chapel*, and thence went home, leaving the remainder of his Duty to be performed by the *Bishop* of *London*.

At the *King's* approach to the *Altar*, the *Bishop* of *Ely* delivered unto Him Bread, and Wine, which He there offered, and then returned to the *Fald ftool*, on the *South* ſide of the *Altar*, near His *Chair* of *State*; before which He kneeled down, and laid His Crown upon the

the *Cushion* before Him, towards His right Hand; and the *Scepter* with the *Dove*, on His left; and gave again to Mr. *Howard* the *Scepter* with the *Cross*, who held it, kneeling on the *King's* right Hand: the *Grand Officers*, and the *Noble-men*, with the four *Swords* naked, and erect, standing about Him.

Then the *Bishop* of *London* said this *Prayer*,

> *Bless, O Lord, we beseech thee, these thy Gifts, and sanctifie them unto this holy Use, &c.*

At the end of which, the Lord *Cornwallis*, *Treasurer* of the *Houshold*, delivered another *Wedg* of *Gold* (which goeth under the name of the *Mark* of *Gold*) to the *Lord Great-Chamberlain*, who presenting it to the *King*, He offered it into the *Bason*, kneeling still at His *Fald-stool*, whil'st the *Bishop* of *London* said the following *Prayer*, beginning thus;

> *Almighty God, give Thee the Dew of Heaven, and the Fatness of the Earth, and abundance of Corn, and Wine, &c.*

And next pronounced this Blessing,

> *Bless, O Lord, the virtuous carriage of this* K I N G, *and accept the Work of His Hands, &c.*

Then the *Bishop* proceeded to the Consecration of the *Sacrament* : which being finished, he first of all received; next, the *Dean* of *Westminster*; then, the *Bishop* of *Bath* and *Wells*; and lastly, the *Bishop* of *Duresm*.

These four *Prelates* having communicated, and Preparation made for the *King's* Receiving (who kneeled all this while before the *Fald-stool*) the *Bishop* of *London* gave the *King* the *Bread*, and the *Dean* of *Westminster* the *Cup*.

As soon as the *King* had received, this *Anthem* was begun by the upper *Quire*.

> *O hearken unto the voice of my Calling, my King, and my God, &c.*

In the mean while, the King returned to His *Throne* upon the *Theatre*, with the *Crown* on His Head, and bearing the *Scepters* in His Hands.

When

When He came thither, He first put off His *Crown*, and delivered it to the *Lord Great-Chamberlain*: then the *Scepter* with the *Cross* to Mr. *Howard*; and that other with the *Dove* to the *Duke* of *Albemarle*.

After this the *Bishop* of *London* went on with the *Communion*; which being finished, the *King* (attended as before) descended from His *Throne* crowned, with both the *Scepters* in His Hand, (the rest of the *Regalia* being carried before Him; and thence proceeded into Saint *Edward's Chapel*, where He took off Saint *Edward's Crown*, and delivered it to the Bishop of *London*; who immediately laid it upon Saint *Edward's Altar*, all the rest of the *Regalia* being given into the hands of the *Dean* of *Westminster*, and laid there also. Then He retired into a Traverse, where He was disrobed of the Robes He was crowned in, which were delivered to the *Dean* of *Westminster* to lay up with the rest of *Regalia*) and invested with His Royal Robes of Purple Velvet, He came near to Saint *Edward's Altar*, where the *Bishop* of *London* standing ready with the *Imperial Crown* in his hands, set that upon His Head. All which being performed, He took the *Scepter* with the *Cross* in His right Hand, and the *Globe* in His left; and proceeded to *Westminster-Hall*, the same way that He came; and attended after the same manner, saving that the *Noble-men*, and *Bishops*, who brought the *Regalia* to the *Abbey Church*, went not now immediately before Him, as they did then, but were ranked in places according to their Degrees: all the *Noble-men* having their *Coronets*, and *Caps* on their Heads; and the *Kings* of *Arms* their *Coronets*.

The *Proceeding* being entred into *Westminster-Hall*, the *Nobility*, and others, who had Tables asigned them, went, and placed themselves thereat; but the *King*, (attended with the *Great Officers*) with-drew into the *Inner-Court* of *Wards*, for half an hour.

In the mean time, all the *Tables* in the Body of the *Hall* were served; *viz.* before the *King's Service* came up, and were placed in this manner.

1. On the right hand (*viz.* the *South-East* side of the *Hall*) were set two *Tables*, one beneath the other: at the upper end of the first (which had two *Side-Tables* to serve it) sate the *Bishops*; and below them the *Judges*, with the rest of the *Long-Robe*.

2. At the second *Table* (which had two *Side-board Tables* likewise to serve it) sate the *Masters* of the *Chancery* and the *Six Clerks*. At which likewise the *Barons* of the *Cinque-Ports* were then necessitated to sit (by reason of a Disturbance which some of the *King's* Footmen made in offering to take the *Canopy* from them) although the upper end of the first *Table* was appointed for them.

On

On the other side of the *Hall* was placed likewise a long Table,   3.
which reached down near to the *Common-Pleas-Court*, whereat the
Nobility dined.

And behind this, close to the Wall, at a shorter Table, sate the
Lord Maior, Aldermen, Recorder, and twelve chief *Citizens of London.*

Lastly, within the *Court of Common-Pleas* was a Table set for the
Officers at Arms, whereat they also dined. Each Table being furnished
with three *Courses* answerable to that of the *King's,* besides the *Banquet.*

At the upper end of the *Hall* (where, upon an ascent of Steps,
a *Theatre* was raised for His *Majestie's* Royal Seat at this great Solemnity) a large Table being placed, the *Serjeant* of the *Ewry,* two
Serjeants at Arms with their *Maces* going before him, bringing up
the *Covering,* was spread by the *Gentlemen-Ushers,* and *Serjeant* of the
Ewry.

This being done, the *Officers* of the *Pantry,* with two *Serjeants at
Arms* also before them, brought up the *Salt of State,* and *Caddinet.*

A little before the *King* returned to Diner, two *Esquires* of the
Body, took their Seats upon two little Foot-stools, on either side of
the Foot of the *King's Chair,* (placed opposite to the middle of the
Table) and there sate until the *King* came in to Diner; when rising,
and performing their Duty in placing the *King's Robes* for His better conveniency of sitting, they sate down again at the *King's* Feet
some part of Diner-time, until the *King* gave them leave to rise.

On the right Side of the *Throne* was erected a *Gallery* for the *Officers at Arms.* And opposite to that, on the other side, another for
the *Musick :* and below, on the old Scaffolds, next the *Court of Common Pleas,* stood the *King's Trumpeters.*

The Proceeding at carrying up of the First Course
to the KING'S TABLE.

The two *Clerks Comptrollers,*
The two *Clerks* of the *Green Cloth,*
And the *Cofferer* of His *Majestie's Houshold.*

All in Black Velvet Gowns, trimm'd with Black Silk, and Gold
Lace, with Velvet Caps raised in the Head.

Six *Serjeants* at *Arms,* two and two.

                                                        The

The *Earl-Marſhal*   The *Lord-High-*   The *Lord High Conſtable*
on the left Hand.   *Steward.*   on the right Hand.

All three mounted on Horſe-back in their Robes, and with their
Coronets on their Heads; having their Horſes richly trapped.

Six *Serjeants* at *Arms*, two and two.

The *Comptroller* of the *Houſhold*, The *Treaſurer* of the *Houſhold*,
with their White Staves.

Earl of *Dorſet*, Sewer.
Earl of *Cheſterfield*, his Aſſiſtant.
The *Knights* of the *Bath*, carrying up the Service, two and two to
a Diſh, which was ſet upon the Table by the *Earl* of *Lincoln* Carver,
aſſiſted by the *Earl*-Sewers.
In the Rear came up the three Clerks of His *Maieſtie's* Kitchin,
all ſuted in Black, Fugar'd, Satin Gowns, and Velvet Caps, in faſhion
like thoſe worn by the Clerks Comptrollers.
Diner being ſet on the Table, the *King* came forth from the *Inner-
Court* of *Wards*, in His *Royal Robes*, with the *Crown* on His Head, and
Scepter in His Hand, having the three *Swords* born naked before
Him, and having waſh'd, ſate down to Diner, the *Biſhop* of *London*
ſaying Grace.
On the *King's* right Hand, the *Noble-men*, that carried the three
Swords, ſtood, holding them naked, and erected, all the Diner-while;
at His left Hand ſtood the *Lord High-Chamberlain*, to whom the *King*
had given the *Scepter* to hold. And at the Table's end, on the *King's*
left Hand, ſate the *Duke* of Y o r k, in his Robes, and Coronet.
Soon after Diner was begun, the Lord *Allington*, by virtue of his
tenure of the *Manor* of *Wymundeley*, in the County of *Hertford*, ſer-
ved the *King* of His firſt *Cup* (which was of *Silver Gilt*) and after
the *King* had drank, he had the *Cup* for his *Fee*.
Next, *Thomas Leigh* Eſquire was brought up to the Table with
a Meſs of *Pottage*, called *Dillegrout*, by reaſon of his tenure of the *Manour* of *Addington*, in the County of *Surrey*.
Afterwards, a little before the ſecond Courſe was ready, Sir *Edward Dymock* Knight (being the *King's* *Champion*, as being ſeized of
the *Manor* of *Scrivelsby*, in the County of *Lincoln*) entred the *Hall*
on a goodly White Courſier, armed at all Points : and there having
made a ſtand for ſome time, advanced in maner following ;

First,

First, Two *Trumpets*.
Then the *Serjeant-Trumpeter* with his Mace.
After him two *Serjeants* at *Arms*, with their Maces.

Then one *Esquire* carrying his *Target*, having his *Arms* depicted thereon; and

Another *Esquire* carrying the *Champion's Lance* upright.

After them Y O R K-Herald at *Arms*.

The *Earl-Marshal*   The *Champion*.   The *Lord High-Constable*
on his left Hand.   on his right Hand.

Both likewise on Horseback.

Being come on some few steps, he made a stand : whereupon the said Herald proclaimed his *Challenge* in these following words;

IF any *Person of what degree soever, high or low, shall deny, or gain-say Our* Sovereign *Lord* King C H A R L E S the Second, *King of* England, Scotland, France, *and* Ireland, Defender of the Faith, *Son and next Heir to Our* Sovereign *Lord* C H A R L E S the First, *the last King deceased, to be right Heir to the Imperial Crown of this Realm of* England; *or that He ought not to enjoy the same :* here is His *Champion, who saith, that he lyeth, and is a false* Traytor, *being ready in person to Combate with him, and in this Quarrel will adventure his Life against him, on what day soever he shall be appointed.*

Whereupon the *Champion* threw down his *Gantlet*, which lying some small time, and no body taking it up, it was delivered unto him again by the same Herald. Then he advanced further forward, until he came to the middle of the *Hall*; where the Herald having reiterated the same Proclamation, the *Gantlet* was again thrown down, taken up, and returned unto him. And lastly, advancing to the Foot of the Steps to the *Throne of State*, the said *Herald* again proclaimed the same *Challenge*, whereupon the *Champion* threw down his *Gantlet* again, which no body taking up, it was delivered unto him.

This being done, the *Earl* of *Penbroke* and *Montgomery* (assisted, as before) presented on the Knee to the *King* a Gilt *Cup* with a Cover, full of Wine, who drank to the *Champion*; and, by the said *Earl* sent him the *Cup*, which having received, he, after three Reverences, drank it all off, went a little backward, and so departed out of the *Hall*, taking the said *Cup* for his Fee.

D d   All

All which being performed, *Garter* Principal King of *Arms*, with the two Provincial Kings of *Arms*, having their Coronets on their Heads; and likewise all the *Heralds*, and *Purfuivants* at *Arms*, came down from the Gallery, and went to the lower end of the Tables, where they made their firft obeyfance to His *Majefty*. Then advancing up into the midft of the Hall, they did the like, and afterwards at the Foot of the Steps towards His *Majeftie's* Throne, where *Garter* being afcended, proclaimed His *Majeftie's* Stile in *Latine*, *French*, and *Englifh*, according to antient ufage, crying *Largefs* thrice. Which done, they all retired backward into the midft of the *Hall*; and there, after crying *Largefs* again thrice, he proclaimed the *King's* Style as before. And laftly, they went yet backwards to the end of the faid *Noble-mens* Table, and did the fame again; and from thence into the *Common-Pleas-Court*, to Diner.

Immediately after this, the fecond Courfe was brought up by the *Gentlemen-Penfiouers*, with the former Solemnity; the laft Difh being carried up by *Erafmus Smith* Efquire, who then prefented the *King* with three *Maple Cups*, on the behalf of *Robert Barnham* Efq; in refpeet of his tenure of the *Manor* of *Nether-Bilfington* in the County of *Kent*, by performance of that fervice on the Day of the *King's Coronation*.

Laftly, the *Lord Maior* of *London* then prefented the *King* with Wine in a *Golden Cup*, having a Cover; of which the *King* having drank, the faid *Lord Maior* received it for his Fee.

By this time the day being far fpent, the *King* (having Water brought Him by the Earl of *Penbroke*, and his Afsiftants) wafhed, and rofe from Diner before the third Courfe was brought in; and, retiring into the *Inner-Court* of *Wards*, He there difrobed Himfelf: and from thence went privately to His *Barge*, which waited for Him at the *Parliament-Stairs*, and fo to the *Privy-Stairs* at *White-Hall*, where He landed.

It is a thing very memorable, that, towards the end of *Diner*-time (although all the former part of the day, and alfo the preceding day, in which the *King* made His *Cavalcade* through *London*, were the onely fair days, that we enjoyed of many both before, and after) it began to *Thunder* and *Lighten* very fmartly: which, however fome fort of People were apt to interpret as *ominous*, and *ill-boding*, yet it will be no difficult matter to evidence from Antiquity, that Accidents of this nature, though happily they might aftonifh, and amaze the common Drove of men, were by the moft Prudent, and Sagacious, look'd upon as a *profperous*, and *happy prefage*. And of this *Virgil* gives

us

us a very pertinent Example (in the eighth Book of his *Æneids*) where *Evander* having addressed himself in a Speech to *Æneas* for aid against the *Hetrurians*, and He being sollicitous how to answer his request, mark what Sign was immediately sent from Heaven.

> *Námque improvisò vibratus ab Æthere fulgor*
> *Cum sonitu venit,* &c.

For suddenly from Heav'n a brandish'd Flash
With Thunder came, *&c.*

And presently after the *Poet* adds,

> *Obstupuère animis alii, sed* Troius *Heros*
> *Agnovit sonitum, & Divæ promissa Parentis.*

While others stood amaz'd, the *Hero* knew
His Mother's Promise by the Sound that flew.

The same *Author*, in another place *, mentions the same thing   * Lib. 2. as a Testimony of *Prayers* heard, and answered ; as when Old *Anchises*, seeing the *lambent Flame* upon his Grand-Child *Iulus* his Head, lifted up his Hands to Heaven, and prayed to *Jove* for help, and direction, he was thus answered,

> *Vix ea fatus erat Senior, subitóque fragore*
> *Intonuit lævum,* &c,

Scarce had the grave Sire spoke, when suddenly
It thundered prosperous, *&c.*

For so *Intonuit lævum* is interpreted by *Servius*, according to the Maxim of the Antient *Augurs*, who interpret *Thunder* from the *North*, that is (as they, contrary to the common *Astronomers*, accounted it) the left part of Heaven, for a prosperous *Omen*.

But, in reference to our present Purpose, we may proceed to a larger Interpretation, and conclude, that the Heavens, with Vollies of *Thunder*, and nimble Flashes of *Lightning*, seemed to give a *Plaudite*, and Acclamation, to this Grand and Sacred *Solemnity* ; in like manner as we Mortals use to close our greater Triumphs with Fire-works, Bonfires, and the loud Report of our great Ordnance :
                                                                                    this

this Terreſtrial Thunder being but the Imitator, and Counterfeit of
the Heavenly Artillery.

* Claud. de
Conſ. Probi-
ni & Olybrii
ver. 205.
And ſo I obſerve it expounded by *Claudian* in theſe Verſes *,

> *Ut ſceptrum geſſere manu, membrisque rigentes*
> *Aptavēre togas, Signum dat ſummus hiulcâ*
> *Nube Pater, gratámque facem per inane rotantes*
> *Proſpera vibrati ſonuerunt Omina Nimbi.*

> As ſoon as rob'd, and ſcepter'd, *Jove* aloud
> His Signal Favour thunders from a Cloud,
> Succeſsful Lightning through Heav'n's Arches ſhines ;
> Both at His Coronation happy Signs.

F I N I S.